D1643949

SHIPWRECKS OF THE ISLE OF WIGHT

SHIPWRECKS
OF THE
ISLE OF WIGHT

by

Ken Phillips

DAVID & CHARLES
Newton Abbot   London   North Pomfret (VT)

British Library CIP Data

Phillips, Kenneth
   Shipwrecks of the Isle of Wight.
   1. Shipwrecks—England—Isle of Wight
   —History
   I. Title
   363.1'23'094228   G525

   ISBN 0–7153–8816–9

Photoset and printed in Great Britain by
Redwood Burn Limited, Trowbridge, Wiltshire
for David & Charles plc
Brunel House, Newton Abbot, Devon

Published in the United States of America
by David & Charles Inc
North Pomfret   Vermont 05053   USA

Where lies the land to which the ship would go?
Far, far ahead, is all her seamen know.
And where the land she travels from? Away,
Far, far behind, is all that they can say.

A. H. Clough. (1819–61)

Front cover
HMS Eurydice at the moment of capsizing with all canvas set in 1878. A reconstruction specially painted for this book by Robert Scott. (Colour transparency by Frank Taylor)

Previous pages
Underley breaking up and almost gone (A. J. Butler and R. G. McInnes). Her story is told on page 67.

Contents

The loss of the *Clarendon* at Blackgang in 1836, from a small watercolour by 'H.D.', painted circa 1870 (Carisbrooke Castle Museum). Her wreck has become part of Island folklore

Foreword

by Dr David Tomalin,
Isle of Wight County Archaeologist

Stories of ships are like ships themselves. If nobody takes care of them, they are well regarded for a while and then, very soon, they are lost.

Information on Island shipwrecks is to be gained from three main sources. Documentary accounts of ship losses on the Island's coast can be traced backwards for the past six hundred years to the opening of the fourteenth century. In the year 1301-2 we find the King's Constable, William Russell, and the local landowner, Adam de Compton, haggling over the spoils of the late ship 'Caleys' which had broken her back on the rocks at Compton. As our colleague Father Hockey astutely observes, there is no mention of survivors or a dispute of ownership in this document (Hockey 1982, 110-111).

The researches of Father Hockey on events such as these during the fourteenth and fifteenth centuries provide an appropriate prelude to the shipwrecks described in the following pages. The earlier accounts, often written in Latin, tell us much of contemporary Island avarice and opportunism. Walter de Goditon and his cronies, when standing before a jury in Southampton on 8 June 1313, had audaciously re-moved some 57 casks of white wine from the *Sainte Marie* after she had been wrecked in Chale Bay. To organise shore-line theft on such a large scale, Walter (of Gotten, Chale) was clearly a man of consider-able resource and we can now recognise him as an early figure in a whole cast of South Wight landowners who were to enter and domi-nate the stage on the occasion of any adventitious wreck. In a Trilogy of Greed in chapter 1 of the following pages, we may find instant deja vu when the old Goditon scenario is played out again some three and a half centuries later by the Bowermans of Brook as they descend upon the wave-borne wreckage of another hapless French wine ship. Shoulder to shoulder on the wet shingle in the early morning mist at Hanover Point, the Bowermans and their henchmen from the Manor of Brook are a match for any law officer and indeed any one who approaches their covetable stack of plump wooden casks.

Like the Knighton Court proceedings of AD 1301, the Bowerman litigation of 1670 is yet another happy historian's windfall whereby the bare facts concerning a shipwreck event are written down for posterity by the quill of the court clerk. In all records such as these the human folly, the bravery, heroism and indeed the entire drama of the wreck is entirely lacking and it is only on the occasion of a major military disaster such as the loss of the *Mary Rose* in 1545 that we are able to glean just a few lines of descriptive narrative.

A turning point in the documentation of Isle of Wight shipwrecks occurs in the mid-eighteenth century when courts martial records of naval losses were kept. The loss, on the Needles, of the *Assurance*, a 40-gun ship returning from Jamaica in 1753, is well documented by this means, likewise the frigate *Pomone* which was wrecked at virtually the same spot on 14 October 1811. In a number of respects the loss of *Assurance* and *Pomone* provide a landmark in the understanding of Island shipwrecks, not least in regards to their documentation. The court martial accounts follow a conventional dry and legal formula but concurrent with *Pomone*'s loss is a report of an entirely new nature as seen through the eyes of the first generation of journalists. The writer in this case is a reporter for the *Salisbury and Winchester Journal*, the earliest of the local provincial newspapers to concern the Isle of Wight. First published as the *Salisbury Journal* as early as 1729, this publication extended its title in 1772 at which time it was also joined by a new rival entitled the *Hampshire Chronicle*. In 1799 these two local newspapers were joined by the *Hampshire Telegraph*, after which were to follow the *Southampton Luminary etc* (1822), the *Southampton Herald and Isle of Wight Gazette* (1823) and the *Hampshire Independent, Isle of Wight and South of England Advertiser* (1835). In 1877 *The News* was published in Portsmouth as the first local daily paper. It was followed in Southampton in 1888 by the *Southern Echo*.

By the late nineteenth century the above range of mainland publications had been joined by a plethora of Isle of Wight weekly newspapers (mostly short-lived) beginning with the *Ryde Visitor* of 1839 and followed notably by the *Isle of Wight Observer* (1845) and the *Isle of Wight County Press* in 1884. The full array of these popular Island newspapers has been summarised by Parker (1975).

It is in the milieu of popular reporting during the nineteenth century that much of this current book has been researched. Such reports readily provide the human element so sadly lacking in the earlier documented accounts, but with such reporting comes all the ambiguity, exaggeration and innuendo so readily nurtured by the newspaper industry. With the sinking of *Lotus* at Rocken End in 1862 we are treated through the pages of the *Isle of Wight Observer* to a vision of reeling wreck-hunters amassed around a newly-opened rum cask whilst from the disintegrated ship we are reminded that only two of the fourteen persons aboard were saved. It is in a scene such as this that we should recall the Goditons and the Bowermans of the past, but we would nevertheless be wrong in accepting without question the implicit suggestion that loss of life on one hand was necessarily related to the acquisition of spirit of another kind well clenched in the other.

Throughout the war years of the present century detailed reports of any kind concerning ship losses are virtually absent. These periods are seemingly well suited to the activities of the oral historian, yet sadly all attempts in this direction have so far failed. This then is our second line of shipwreck research, which through the media of professional television and radio interview will serve future shipwreck events but has yet to be gainfully employed in retrieving the recent past. The loss of the *Cuba* (11,000 tons) on 6 April 1945 clearly marks a disaster of considerable magnitude, yet nothing is known of the fate of the large body of men on board. Perhaps even more surprising is the lack of eye-witness accounts of the Island's own ferry the *Portsdown* which was blown in two by a mine whilst leaving Portsmouth Harbour on 20 September 1941. Of the twenty-four persons saved, a number were doubtless Islanders, yet not a single witness of the event has yet been interviewed. The need for a local archive for oral records such as these is clearly apparent.

The third means of island shipwreck research is to be found on the seabed itself. In this respect the term 'ship loss' is indeed a misleading one, for both the salvage diver and the marine archaeologist are well aware that a ship can never be totally destroyed and that it must eventually settle on the ocean floor to become a tiny monument to man's endeavours entombed in the sands of time.

Underwater exploration of the Isle of Wight seabed began at a remarkably early date with the loss of the *Mary Rose* in 1545. Within twelve days of the disaster Charles Brandon, Duke of Suffolk, had provided a list of salvage requirements including 'thirty Venetian maryners and one Venetian carpenter'. Also 'sixty English maryners to attend upon them' (Rule 1983, 40). The Venetian mariners were clearly charged with specialised work which seemingly included free-diving at low water to attach cables to the sunken hull. Such a lung dive, Margaret Rule observes, would be well within the capabilities of a Mediterranean sponge fisherman. It is perhaps no coincidence that the payments made in 1547 and 1549 for the successful recovery of guns were made to an Italian, one Peter Paul.

An important landmark in the development of diving technology is the loss, during the reign of Charles I, of the Dutch East Indiaman *Campen*, on The Needles of the Isle of Wight. Running from a storm on 14 October 1627, *Campen* bottomed on the chalk wave-cut plat-form in Scratchells Bay where she was very soon to disintegrate. Soon Robert Newland, a merchant of Newport, was busy with the aid of local fishermen grappling in the traditional manner with tongs over the wreck site. By the following summer, however, Newland, no doubt much to his surprise, was upstaged by the arrival of the Dutch-man, Jacob Johnson, who was equipped both with his own vessel and a prototype diving bell (Larn *et al.* 1985).

Throughout the summer of 1628 the Dutchman, commonly known as 'Jacob the Diver', was generally successful in recovering anchors, ordnance and notable quantities of lead ingots and silver bullion. Working the primitive diving bell was not, however, without its physiological hazards, for Jacob also records that his ears bled (Rod-die 1976).

A further pioneer event in diving history was to occur in Island waters almost a century later with the disastrous loss of the *Royal George* on 29 August 1782. In the following year William Tracey, another pioneer of underwater salvage, entered into a contract to raise the ship but he was soon to discover that the adversity of the cold Solent water was as nothing compared with the inventive inertia of the Navy Board which was to use every bureaucratic device to impede his work. Effectively bankrupted and crippled through diving, Tracey was forced to abandon the task which was eventually taken up some 50 years later by the inventive Deane brothers of Deptford. Between 1836 and 1839 John and Charles Deane raised 29 guns from the *Royal*

George wreck whilst working concurrently on the rediscovered wreck of the *Mary Rose*. Sadly the bronze guns recovered from the *Royal George* were promptly melted down to become the basal fittings of Nelson's Column (Medland 1986) but it is interesting to observe that the three bronze pieces as well as the iron guns recovered by the Deanes from the *Mary Rose* were already considered to be of sufficient antiquity to warrant preservation.

In terms of understanding the maritime history and archaeology of Isle of Wight waters, the good fortune accompanying the salvage enterprises of Johnson and the Deanes can now only be viewed as ill-fortune when weighed against current public expectations of museum management and heritage conservation. The line which divides salvage operations from scientific underwater archaeology is a fundamental one and it is most important in any book dealing with the topic of shipwreck that this line should be clearly drawn. At a time when cargoes of historic artefacts have received widespread publicity on television and in the auction room, it is clear that in the interests of quick profit a deliberate blurring of this line is taking place and that it can be readily assisted by high quality popular publications which present sea-bed booty as 'archaeology'. In any fundamental test to distinguish scientifically motivated excavation from plunder, the discriminating reader should always seek the detailed published site plans showing the whole of the sea-bed evidence as well as the name of the accredited museum in which the full collection of artefacts is housed.

In following the shipwreck episodes set out in this book it is inevitable that we should ask what has become of the sea-bed evidence of the craft concerned. Fortunately a number have been examined by Martin Woodward, and it is as a result of his efforts that a selection of artefacts from the later ships, including the *Alcester, Boxer, Highland Brigade*, and *HMS Hazard* can now be seen in the Bembridge Maritime Museum.

It is in dealing with the sea-bed remains of earlier vessels in Island waters that the need for greater archaeological understanding arises. Man's use of the Solent covers some 7000 years during which craft of prehistoric date would most certainly have plied this important channel. The boat ballast of Isle of Wight limestone found in a burial mound of c. 1500 BC in South Dorset offers incontestible evidence of Early Bronze Age sailings (Tomalin 1984) whilst an anchor of Pur-

15

beck Limestone recovered from the western Solent is a reminder of a similar West Country voyage in Roman times (Tomalin 1987).

Without doubt one of the most notable sea-bed discoveries is the evidence for Roman shipping recently found in Yarmouth Roads. Here a scatter of fragments of early amphorae found at a depth of some 16 metres attests the arrival in our waters of a Roman wine ship some time before the birth of Christ (Tomalin 1987). It is in dealing with Island sites such as Yarmouth Roads that the enormity of our true responsibilities becomes clearly apparent, for sites such as these are by no means insulated from any imminent threat by a cosy jacket of water. The popularity of sub-aqua sport diving is now so widespread over Southern England that Isle of Wight waters to a depth of 40m are readily accessible to large numbers of visitors many of whom may have a very casual attitude towards sea-bed antiquities. The remains of ancient craft, moreover, can be very lightly buried on the seabed where they are highly vulnerable to certain means of trawling as well as to tidal scour. Currently areas of the Island seabed are subject to both trawling and gravel extraction and this, along with sport diving, lays considerable but very often unrecognised responsibilities on all concerned. If the heritage is to survive the advance of technology, these are all challenges which clearly must be taken up and we should take some heart from the policy of the Isle of Wight County Archaeological Unit which has extended its Sites and Monuments Record to the sea-bed terrain. By this means local authorities may be better informed on the archaeological implications of sea-bed mineral extraction licences whilst sport divers may be personally advised on the significance of their discoveries.

In the personal testimonies of shipwrecked officers and crew to be found in the following pages we can glean, amid the chaos, a little of the process by which a ship is broken up and reduced to what the archaeologist might describe as a sea-bed assemblage. This process of ship degradation is an important one and it presents an area where amateur divers in their future exploration on sites of documented wrecks have a vital role to play. By restraining the immediate thirst for souvenirs and by carefully mapping the position of all of the seabed debris it is possible to reconstruct the various means by which a wooden ship may eventually disintegrate. This task has been attempted on the protected wreck of the *Pomone* on the Goose Rock site at the Needles, and it is here that archaeologists have come to understand that even with the total disintegration of a ship's hull the sinking and settling of its components can yet follow a meaningful order. In following Captain Haws' personal experience in the shuddering hulk of the *Alcester* we are given a first-hand account of the apparent chaos of the shipwrecking process yet on the site of *Pomone*'s sea-bed grave the archaeological team have been able to demonstrate from the distribution of brass buttons that even the marines' spare uniforms eventually came to rest no further than a few metres from the site of their former cabins.

In 1986 a charitable body, the Isle of Wight Archaeological Committee, with the aid of the Manpower Services Commission, the Isle of Wight County Council and Mr. & Mrs. Trevor Green of Oxford, set up a maritime archaeological group at Porte La Salle, Yarmouth, where underwater excavation and sea-bed archaeological data is currently being pursued by a team of twenty-three personnel. It is hoped that the discoveries of this team will soon be presented in such a manner that every visitor to the Isle of Wight can share in the exhilaration of shipwreck exploration and research. In the meantime this book undoubtedly provides us with a new view of our Island's shipwreck history. In the remote windswept churchyard in the village of Chale we can look upon the sad weathered slabs covering the *Clarendon* and *Lotus* tombs with a new sense of perspective as we come to realise the enormity of the number of ill-documented ships of earlier years which have come to grief on the same stretch of coast.

On the coastal footpath at Rocken End we are reminded by the author of the reeling rum revellers climbing, on 17 October 1862, the narrow beach path from the wreck of the *Lotus*. Finally having learned of the aftermath of the wrecking of the *Cedarine* and of the hedgerows populated by intoxicated felons and soldiers we really cannot take a truly sober look at the village of Brighstone ever again.

17

Introduction

Around the Isle of Wight modern wrecks are rare: conversely, detailed local reports earlier than the beginning of the nineteenth century are almost as scarce. It is from the years between 1800 and the First World War, with their voluminous newspaper accounts, that I have garnered the greater part of this work. Obviously, it is impossible to recount in full the many hundreds of wrecks we know in the waters of the Wight; a few must stand witness for them all. Some will be familiar to the readers, some will not, but all in some small measure have contributed to our maritime heritage. Their inclusion here stands only on that premise.

The chapter of war losses was certainly the most frustrating to write. The normal day to day reporting processes had ceased and ship losses around the shores of Britain went unremarked or, when obviously public knowledge, subject to censorship. What is more, the smoke screen of secrecy is not yet fully blown away.

To achieve a desirable uniformity when discussing sailing vessels of different periods and using various reports of differing quality and origins, all spellings and terms are as given by the invaluable 'Country Life Book of Nautical Terms under Sail'. However, the word 'ship' is often used in its widest sense, to avoid repetitive use of brig, brigantine, barque, etc, even though the vessel in question may not have been ship rigged.

An important point that requires some clarification is that of size. Most reports merely state that a ship was of so many tons, but unless the word ton is qualified it is meaningless. For many centuries the method of assessing a ship's size was based on the premise that all were similar. That is to say that the ratio of beam to length and depth was more or less constant. For tax and revenue purposes the difference between one ship and another was solely in the weight or volume of cargo carried. This, calculated as the load between a ships light and full load draught, was expressed in tons burden or burthen, or sometimes Builder's Tonnage. After 1836 this was called Builders Old

Measure and the capacity of a ship was from then on calculated at 92.4 cubic feet per ton; this was entitled New Measurement. The formula was again altered in 1854 to 100 cubic feet per gross ton, which it still is.

While we are on the subject the reader might like to be reminded of net tons, deadweight tons and displacement tons, the metric tonne of 2204.62 lbs, and of course the freight ton, which can be either 40 cubic feet or 2240 lbs, depending on which of the two gives the shipowner most profit. We must not forget the rating of a container ship in TEU's; short for Twenty feet Equivalent Units. The policy adopted here is to quote ship tonnages as they were given in the contemporay reports.

1

Right of Wreck –
A Trilogy of Greed

In these days of instant communication a vessel in distress has only to radio for assistance and it is immediately forthcoming. Whatever the weather help will be at hand and we tend to accept the dedication of the rescue services without question. Yet life saving at sea, as we understand it, is a comparitively modern phenomenon. Until about the middle of the nineteenth century no organisation dedicated solely to that end existed. But hard on the heels of the development of the first true lifeboat by Henry Greathead in the last decade of the eighteenth century came the founding of the National Institution for the Preservation of Life from Shipwreck in 1824, later re-formed into the now familiar Royal National Life-boat Institution.

In the Isle of Wight by 1860 the first lifeboat went into service at Brook, paid for by public subscription in response to a growing awareness of loss of life from shipwreck on the Island's coast. The first lifeboat at Bembridge, named *City of Worcester* followed in 1867. For hundreds of years, until the advent of the National Institution, shipwrecks had been seen mainly as an opportunity for profit.

Since the fourteenth century the law had permitted the owner of a shipwrecked vessel to recover his goods if he claimed them within three months of their salvage, but added the proviso that a man or a beast must have escaped alive from the wreck. That was a very convenient loophole. How many times did interested parties, eager to get their hands on the cargo, ensure that the essential condition was not fulfilled? No doubt there were sometimes selfless humanitarian acts, but we know too that human life was sacrificed for greed, because as early as 1224 the Bishop of Winchester, Peter des Roches, had decreed the excommunication of any man who for personal gain prevented the shipwrecked from saving themselves. What is more, the bishop ordered his threat to be proclaimed at least three times a year in the Island churches. There may not have been deliberate murder of survivors but how many perished for the want of a friendly hand withheld when most needed?

Goods unclaimed after a year and a day became the property of the Crown or someone to whom the Crown had granted the right. Three people who held that right on the Isle of Wight are important to our story – Isabella de Fortibus, Richard Worsley and Robert Holmes. Although they span a period of almost four hundred years they each throw light on the importance of shipwreck to different sections of the community. For although they held the right it did not go un-challenged by the lower social orders if they could get to the beach first.

Isabella de Fortibus actually owned the Isle of Wight in the thir-teenth century, but according to King Edward I that did not auto-matically give her 'right of wreck'. As the profits from shipwreck constituted a very important element of royal income the king was angered at her insistence that it did and he summoned her to answer a writ of Quo Warranto before judges at Winchester in 1280.

Isabella's case was that 'she and all her ancestors from the time of King Richard, and also before that time always unto the present time, have had their wreck of the sea in her fee in the Isle of Wight without any interruption', while the King's case was founded on the fact that Isabella's brother, Baldwin de Insula, had appropriated to his own benefit all proceeds from shipwrecks around the Island without the assent and will of the King. Because Isabella was her brother's heir she could not claim what he had taken unlawfully.

The jury found for Isabella, declaring that she 'and all her ancestors from the time whereof memory does not exist, and always hereunto had such wreck of the sea in her fee in the Isle of Wight'. The Justices Itinerant had no option but to confirm Isabella in all the rights she had claimed and exercised for so long. But it didn't really matter. In 1293 when she was fifty six years old Isabella de Fortibus died. On her death bed she sold the Isle of Wight to Edward I for a miserable 6,000 marks (about £4,000) so he soon had back the profitable shipwrecks.

Isabella was the last private owner of the Island and with her also died the lordship of the Isle of Wight. It is true the title was used again many times, but as a mere shadow of its former self, conferred only by the Crown and was never again freely held. Administration of the Island passed into the hands of men styled Wardens, a term in use until 1461 when it was superseded by the title 'Captain of the Isle of Wight'. This change probably resulted from the strengthening of the defences of the Island and increasing awareness of its importance to national security.

Richard Worsley held the Captaincy from 1538 until 1553. In 1545 he in person led a fierce and bloody onslaught against a powerful French landing party marauding across the Isle of Wight, driving it back into the sea. The party had been landed from a French fleet under Claude D'Annebault anchored in St Helens roads. It has been conjectured that this was to spur the English into action and that when Henry VIII, then in Portsmouth, saw the smoke rising from burning Island villages he would order the English fleet to join battle. The *Mary Rose* sailing out of Portsmouth to do just that capsized and sank taking almost 400 men before the very eyes of the king. As a result of her discovery and raising she has become not only the Isle of Wight's but also one of the world's most famous wrecks.

Richard Worsley was the son of James Worsley, Keeper of the Wardrobe to Henry VIII. His mother was Anne Leigh, heiress to Appuldurcome estates on the Isle of Wight which he inherited at the death of his father in 1538. At Appuldurcombe in 1540 Richard Worsley entertained King Henry and his powerful minister Thomas Cromwell, so he was a man acquainted with the corridors of power.

At the beginning of March 1544 a ship, the *Conception* was wrecked on the Isle of Wight. We would know nothing of her but for a chance document preserved among the Worsley papers in the Isle of Wight County Record Office. It gives us an insight into the merchandise a Tudor period trading ship might carry and into the procedures by which a man like Worsley profited by her wreck.

The *Conception* was driven ashore near Dunnose Point, close to Shanklin and it would seem that she remained more or less in one piece which permitted Richard Worsley to easily control the wreck site to his advantage. He would certainly have an armed guard placed there to protect what was in the law of the time his absolute right to the

22

wreck, though that probably did not deter some of the local inhabi-tants from little fishing villages prowling about after dark in the hope of a few pickings.

What then was *Conception* carrying in her hold to create such interest in 1544? First on the manifest was that great staple of English trade, wool, woven into broadcloth. The prosperity of England had long been founded on it. The treatment of the cloth, ordered by the traders, after its salvage is a sure indication of its pre-eminent impor-tance to their profits. The agreement is quite specific on the matter: 'and the said Richard shall also cause the said cloth, as well whole as in pieces, to be washed, dried and delivered to the said merchants or their assigns at the quay of the town of Newport within the said Isle at his costs and charges'.

Also in the cargo were cattle hides and calf skins, together with another product of dead animal processing, tallow. Additionally men-tioned are pewter, cotton and kersey, another woollen cloth, rather coarse in texture.

The document finally sets out the profit to be made from the wreck: 'Richard Worsley to have for the recovery and saving of all such merchandise within the said ship . . . to the behoof and profit of us the said merchants and laders, the fourth part for his pains and charges of all the said wares so hereinafter by him saved and recovered the said Richard Worsley delivering or causing to be delivered to us the said merchants or to any assigns the other three parts clear of all costs and charges.'

Reading this agreement it is easy to understand why 'right of wreck' was a zealously guarded privilege.

The third example of a claimant to right of wreck in the Isle of Wight is Sir Robert Holmes, a brilliant commander. Appointed to the newly built *Defiance*, 66 guns, he received his knighthood from Charles II who was present at the ship's launching at Woolwich in 1665, despite the plague then raging.

Commanding the squadron operating on the Dutch coast, Holmes achieved an outstanding success against the Baltic Fleet supposedly secure in its anchorage. With his squadron and a few fireships he entered the channel between the islands of Vlie and Schelling, de-stroyed two men-o'-war, burnt 180 merchant ships and set fire to the town of Brandans. The English casualties were but twelve men killed or wounded. In 1666 Sir Robert Holmes received for his services the governorship of Sandown Castle, followed a year later by appointment as Governor of the Isle of Wight and Commander-in-Chief at Portsmouth. From that time on he resided at Yarmouth, building in the town a splendid house which still stands as the George Inn. There he entertained King Charles II, Prince Rupert, the Duke of York and many other notables. He was master of all he surveyed and certainly claimed the right of wreck. There were some however who disputed that.

One such person was John Bowerman, son of the Lord of the Manor of Brook. The Bowermans were a long established family. The sea formed the southern boundary of their estates and wrecks on that part of the coast they reckoned as Bowerman property. Sooner or later the issue would be contested and in 1670 it was.

On January 4th that year a ship laden with French wines and brandy was wrecked at Hanover Point on Bowerman land and Sir Robert Holmes despatched his officers with all haste to seize the cargo.

An Order in Council by King Charles clearly gave him a right to the wreck, it 'being within the said Vice-Admiralty of the Isle of Wight did properly belong to him as Vice-Admiral' but when the officers arrived at the scene they were met by an uncompromising John Bowerman. The ship had started to break up and about thirty pipes of brandy, together with other goods, had already been removed from the wreck and were stacked along the beach.

A pipe of brandy was 105 gallons and would weight about half a ton. Indeed, cargo ships were measured at the time by the amount of wine it was estimated they could carry; two pipes equalling one ton. The pipe itself was a wooden cask, and when full obviously very awkward to handle, so there must have been a considerable body of strong men standing behind John Bowerman as he watched the approaching agents of law and order.

Holmes's officers approached, according to documents preserved in Carisbrooke Castle, 'in a peaceable manner to salve and preserve the same and take the same into custody but were in a violent manner opposed therein by one John Bowerman and his accomplices who did forbid the officers and did declare that neither they nor Holmes should meddle or make therewith'. But John Bowerman was emphatic that as the ship was wrecked on his father's land the goods were his and the officers left the scene and went back to Yarmouth.

What was Sir Robert Holmes to do? Being a man of action, and a man of power unused to having his orders defied his first reaction must surely have been to take the goods by force. However the only force available at that time was the local militia which had to be mustered from the local population for the defence of the Island in case of invasion. It would be improper to use it now, apart from which the Bowermans were themselves commanders of some of the militia companies and Holmes knew very well where local allegiances would lie. So instead of taking the law into his own hands he appealed directly to King Charles. On January 20th 1670, only sixteen days after the wreck, the King sat in council with his advisers to hear Holmes's petition, a speed of events indicative of Holmes' influence at Court. It was an influence which made certain the royal verdict that the brandy and all the other goods 'be delivered to the custody of the said Vice Admiral or to such officers of the Admiralty as he shall appoint. And hereunto as well, the said Mister Bowerman and all others concerned are required to yield Due Obedience as they and every of them will answer the contrary at their peril'.

How much of the cargo Holmes managed to retrieve is not known. In view of the King's threat, probably most of it. There were at least 3,000 gallons of brandy salvaged from the wreck and it is impossible not to believe that at least a few casks were not spirited away before Holmes got back to the Island with the King's orders. Of the crew of the wrecked ship there appears not a word about their fate. With fifteen tons of brandy at stake, it is doubtful if they were given a second thought.

208

Captain Willson's defect list for *Les Deux Amis* (Public Record Office, Crown Copyright)

2

Where Lies The Land?
– Sailing Ships Ashore

Les Deux Amis 1799

Samuel Willson, Master of His Majesty's Schooner *Les Deux Amis* had only a short voyage to make to Portsmouth from the island of Jersey where his ship then lay, but he had reason for only a short trip, Samuel Willson, not normally a nervous man, was to be most unhappy at the prospect. Earlier that year, 1799, Willson had sailed the schooner to the Channel Islands, but had the misfortune to finish up on the rocks. The vessel was pulled clear and towed into harbour for repairs which were good enough only to enable *Les Deux Amis* to return to Portsmouth.

In Willson's opinion those repairs left the schooner hardly sea-worthy. Going down to his cabin he wrote a list of defects that in his opinion hazarded the safety of the ship. The list could be looked on as a form of insurance against blame to himself if anything went wrong during the passage back to Portsmouth.

Perhaps Willson had the gift of second sight. He wrote:

Les Deux Amis, Schooner

Defects after her being repaired at Jersey

Upon her first being floated 5th May made 2 foot water per hour
Afterwards................................. 18 inches   do.
Forefoot... watching
Sternpost............................... started 3 or 4 inches up
Rudder............................. Hung with only Two Pintles
Broadside..................... Bilged, several timbers being broke.
Keel...................... Of pine, the old one being totally carried
away at Jersey [presumably the false keel]

N.B. Only repaired (by contract after being driven on the rocks at Jersey) to cross the Channel.

Samuel Willson's list demonstrates only too clearly how justified he was to be apprehensive about the coming voyage. When first put into the water after the so called repairs the hull leaked like the proverbial sieve, and, although reduced, eventually, the leak rate was such that in normal circumstances it would be quite unacceptable. The ship would require constant working of the pumps to stay afloat. Such a state of affairs is hardly to be wondered at when we read that several broken timbers at the turn of the bilge were not replaced. One can only assume that such a job was either beyond the capability of the repair dock in Jersey or that the Navy was not prepared to pay a private firm to do it. Perhaps the work could be done more cheaply in the dockyard at Portsmouth. If the schooner could be got there of course.

Another item obviously critical to the wellbeing of the ship was the rudder. Presumably the sternpost being 'started up' three or four inches prevented the rudder from being hung on more than two pintles instead of the usual four or five. With hindsight we can say that this defect probably contributed more than any other to the eventual loss of the ship.

Built in France and fitted out as a privateer carrying 16 guns Les Deux Amis was a thorn in the side of British shipping until December 1796 when she was captured by H.M.S. Polyphemus. On board her when she sailed from Jersey were Messieurs D'Auvergne and Tempriere and Mathew Gosset, Esquire, Viscount of the Island of Jersey.

In company sailed another schooner the *Prince of Auvergne*. Whether this had any connection with M. D'Auvergne is not known, nor is anything about the vessel, except that if she was supposed to stand by the leaking *Les Deux Amis* she was most unsuited to the task, being a much slower and unhandy vessel.

Once safely ashore with time to collect his thoughts, Willson had to write all that he could remember of the events leading to the loss of his ship, and his subsequent actions. The log book had not been saved and the account he compiled, although headed 'Observations on Board, 23rd May 1799', could not have been written on the ship. It is a single coherent narrative, flowing, without hesitation, from its beginning to its end. It is also rather lengthy. From it we can extract the story, piece by piece.

Les Deux Amis sailed from Jersey for Portsmouth on the 22nd of May and despite Willson's migivings the voyage started well enough.

He reported:

First part moderate and clear.
At 1.0.p.m. Set square sail. Out all reefs. Set flying jib.
2.0.p.m. Set foretop sail. Set staysail.
2.30.p.m. Set forestaysail. Set foretopgallant sails.
6.0.p.m. Cape La Hague. 3 to 4 miles.
The *Prince of Auvergne* schooner, being a great way astern, made the signal for her to make more sail which she answered but at 1/2 past 7 lost sight of her.

Conditions now obviously began to deteriorate.

In topgallant sail, down staysail.
8.00 p.m. Light breezes and cloudy
10.00 p.m. In square sail
11.30 p.m. Single reefed topsails
at 12.00 (midnight). Hauled down fore and main sails and flying jib and double reefed them.
2.00 a.m. Fresh breezes and hazey with a heavy swell, the schooner making much water and labouring much.
I judged it expedient to make land as soon as possible and kept on accordingly, I wanted to heave the lead but having none on board made the best I could out of beaten lead but it would not cast with correctness in any depth of water.

The absence of the lead was to give rise to some very close questioning at the subsequent court martial.

> 3.30 a.m. Hove the lead but could not get bottom.
> 4.00 a.m. Hove the lead again but as before could get no ground.
> In a few minutes afterward the loom of the land appearing at some distance under the haze and just under the lee bow put the helm down immediately to get the schooner about as we could not make out what land it was, and just as she was in steerage she struck abaft and knocked her rudder off when immediately she came broadside to the wind and sea.

Mounting the rudder on only two pintles was not a seaworthy job as Willson very well knew. It was the early loss of the rudder that cost Samuel Willson his ship, but, undaunted he fought to save her. His account from this point dramatically describes the efforts and exertions that were typical to save a stranded vessel when time allowed. In so many shipwrecks there was no time.

> I instantly let go the anchor and brought her head to wind, which shifting round more to the southward and it being ebbtide, she continued striking, and lay till the flood had made again, during which time I kept the pumps working in the hopes of freeing her, and firing signals of distress . . .'

Willson's worst fears regarding the broken bilge timbers were fully realised. Water was pouring into the hull faster than the pumps could clear it. But luckily the distress signals were seen and some help was at hand.

> We then carried another anchor out and received some assistance from a small shore boat but all our endeavours to heave her off were ineffectual.

Only desperate measures could now save them.

> I then had the masts cut away by the board to ease her, but finding the water still gaining on us being more than half full not withstanding our labouring at the pumps I was compelled to cut the cables and let her drive higher on the beach, there being a very heavy surf setting on it.

So the fight to save the *Les Deux Amis* was lost but the fight to save her crew was not. A line was got ashore which enabled the ship's boat to be hauled through the boiling sea between the schooner and the beach until all on board were saved, 'although not without difficulty'. Once his crew were safe Samuel Willson, good naval man that he was, turned his attention to the ship's stores, 'taking anything that could be got or which floated on shore, up to the barracks' Then, tired and exhausted though he must have been after his night long exertions, he saw that his men were provided with food and shelter and then turned to the important matter of informing the Admiralty. Willson's account says:

'Got my officers and people housed and victualled at a contiguous farm-houses at 2/6 per man per day, of which I immediatly informed the Victualling Board by letter and wrote to Mr Nepean informing him of the misfortune that had attended His Majesties Schooner and requestiong him to communicate the same to the Lords Commissioners of the Admiralty.'

Samuel Willson ends his report with a short sentence that dismisses in a few words what must have been hours of hard and dangerous work: 'At the high water the schooner was overflown and as the tide fell endeavoured to get on board to preserve the stores and provisions but the heavy surf prevented us.'

The stresses and anxieties of the wreck were over, but ahead loomed the inevitable court martial. But Willson had to write one more letter, this time to Admiral Parker, Commander-in-Chief at Spithead. This was dated May 27th, four days after the loss of *Les Deux Amis*.

Grange Chine, Isle of Wight
27th May 1799

Sir,
It is with the greatest concern I have to represent the loss of His Majesty's Schooner *Les Deux Amis* under my command in the passage from Jersey to Portsmouth at this place on the 23rd instand soon after 4 o'clock in the morning. I have taken the liberty of sending enclosed a copy of the transactions of that unfortunate day as I transmitted the same passport by letter to Mr. Nepean and must request you will attribute my not having sent it to you, instead of to London, at that time to my purturbation of mind and not to any disrespect.'

33

With a court martial pending Samuel Willson could not afford to upset anybody. He would need every friend he could find.

The court martial was convened on board H.M.S. *Gladiator* in Portsmouth harbour on 10th June 1799. The President was Vice Admiral Sir Roger Curtis, Bt. second in command to the C. in C. Twelve captains sat with him and Mr. Greetham, the Judge Advocate for the Navy. After the opening formalities Willson's narrative of the loss of *Les Deux Amis* was read and he was then questioned about it.

The Court Have you any statement respecting the loss of the vessel more than has been read?

Willson No, except an account of her defects. (which was produced).

The Court Have you any complaints to make against any of your officers or people respecting the loss?

Willson I have not.

(**To the Officers and People**)

The Court Do you know of any misconduct on the part of Mr. Willson or any of her People respecting her loss?

Here was a dramatic moment for Samuel Willson. One hostile word and his seagoing career would be finished for ever. But he need not have worried, the answer came firmly enough – No!

Next to be examined was Mr. George Meason, the master's mate.

What, he was asked, became of the schooner's log book? The importance of the ship's log is that as orders are given such as changes of course or change of sail they are noted and form a permanent record of what actually happened and its salvage is always important. The court obviously thought that if Willson could save himself and all his crew he could have saved the log book as well. No subsequent account is ever so trustworthy. Meason's rather lame answer that 'it was lost with the ship' was something the court already knew. The real intention of the question was a warning to other ships' officers that courts martial took a dim view of 'lost' log books and would not lightly accept shipwreck as an excuse.

George Meason was then asked if he knew what distance the vessel had sailed since her clearing Cape La Hague the preceeding evening, until grounding on the Isle of Wight. His answer, 'I do not', was again highly unsatisfactory from a master's mate. In answer to further questioning, he described how he was below decks when the ship ran aground, but instantly came up to find it was broad daylight but very foggy. He was barely able to discern the land, which appeared to him to be about three miles distant. This last remark was absurd, three miles out from Grange Chine would place *Les Deux Amis* well outside the 10 fathom (20 metre) line and a ship of her size would not have drawn more than two fathoms. The five fathom contour is only about three-quarters of a mile offshore so *Les Deux Amis* must have been almost on the beach when she struck and George Meason rushed up on deck. The court made no comment but hot on the scent, turned to the missing sounding lead.

The Court It is stated in the narrative of the loss of the schooner that there was no sounding lead on her. Do you know how she came to leave port without carrying a sounding lead on board?

Meason We had lost our lead in Jersey Road in sweeping for our anchor.

The answer again seemed unsatisfactory, but went unchallenged. Meason finished his testimony by saying he had left the deck at 12 o'clock of the night preceeding the stranding, that is to say about four hours before. The wind had begun to freshen from SSW and thick weather was coming on. In his opinion Mr. Willson, his officers and crew had made every possible exertion to save the ship and stores.

The next witness called was, somewhat surprisingly, a Jersey pilot, Philip De Guichy by name. Why the Jersey pilot was still on board so far from home is difficult to explain, unless of course the weather had been too rough to put him off. How long, he was asked, had he been on deck before *Les Deux Amis* struck ground on the Isle of Wight? Three hours and a half, he replied, and then added, The weather was very thick and blowing a good strong breeze from the WSW. She was going about four knots or four and a half.

The Court During that time how often was the lead hove?

De Guichy I cannot say, but I saw the Commander heave the lead once, but I do not know how often. I asked him if he had got bottom but he said 'no'. I was forward looking out for land.

The Court Was the schooner brought to, to regularly sound?

De Guichy No but she was brought to the wind to deaden her way, but we had the mainsail and foresail down when the lead was hove. She had very little way through the water. After we had sounded she was put to her course again.

The Court Do you know that Mister Willson beat up some lead as a substitute for the sounding lead?

De Guichy No, but there was some lead beaten up which I saw but I did not know who did it.

The Court How far could you see the land?

De Guichy I was windward to look for the Needles, the Commander saw the land under the haze to leeward. I could not see it at first, it was very hazy. I thought we could see about a mile and a half. The first we saw were the breakers at about half a mile.

The Court Did the Commander appear to be anxious?

DeGuichy He was upon deck the whole watch and appeared very anxious for the safety of the King's vessel.

The Court Was the log hove during the night?

De Guichy Yes, twice in the watch.

A log at that period was a wooden board-like device streamed from the stern of a ship. It was secured by a light line in which knots were tied at about every fifty feet although some ship's masters would slightly vary this distance according to their experience of a particular vessel. As the ship sailed away from the log the line ran out and the knots slipping through a seaman's fingers were counted against the run of a thirty second sandglass. This gave the speed of the ship in knots, or nautical miles per hour, thus enabling the distance run to be calculated.

A seaman named Anderson was also asked if the log was used during his watch. He answered, it was every hour. She had gone 30 miles at 12 o'clock upon the log from the time we had set the land. The land in question was Cape de la Hague, from which they had taken their departure.

These persistent enquiries into the sounding lead and the log were of course to establish if faulty navigation was the prime cause of the loss of *Les Deux Amis*. If that were so then perhaps the miserable state of the ship's hull could be glossed over and Captain Willson blamed for everything. He must have been afraid that such a conclusion was one the naval authorities might find it very convenient for the court martial to reach.

Philip De Guichy in his testimony said the wind was from the WSW and that he was looking to windward for the Needles. If that was true *Les Deux Amis* must have been sailing along the Island coast in a westerly direction on a course slightly converging with the shore line and the pilot looking out to sea away from the land. A WSW wind will blow directly on to the shore along that coast of the Wight. Philip De

Guichy also added that the Commander first saw land 'under the haze leeward'. If his word were accepted Willson had every reason to fear the consequences, but De Guichy put the wind direction 45 degrees different to his own master's mate.

But his fears were unfounded. The court rose and when it returned announced its feelings:

> That the loss of His Majesty's Schooner *Les Deux Amis* was caused by her running on shore at the Great [sic] Chine in the Isle of Wight and there wrecked. That no blame whatever is imputable to the said Mister Samuel Willson, her Officers and Company on the occasion, but that every effort was made by them for the safety of the said schooner and for the preservation of her stores and did adjudge them to be acquitted.

No one had raised the question of the ship the Navy ordered home so hastily, so hastily that she had to sail in an unseaworthy condition. But Willson no doubt thought it wiser to return to the quiet obscurity of his sea-going career. He had escaped public blame, if only just, but his own conscience told him he had done his best.

Clarendon 1836

Of all the shipwrecks around the Isle of Wight none is more secure in the corporate folk memory than the loss of the *Clarendon*. Ask any Islander to name a ship wrecked on his shores and before any other he will say the *Clarendon*, even if he does not know the date or the details.

It is difficult to say why the *Clarendon* should be so remembered. She was only a small ship, about 345 tons, and many vessels far larger than her came to grief on the Wight. Perhaps it was the death of almost everyone on board, including young children, that gives her, on a small scale, the aura of a Titanic, and in similar fashion generates a sentimental fascination that seems never to diminish.

Clarendon left St. Kitts, under the command of Captain Samuel Walker, on 27th August 1836. Her cargo was a typical one from the West Indies – sugar, molasses, and rum. In addition to her freight she carried eleven passengers and seventeen crew. Six of the passengers were all one family, a 42-year-old Lieutenant Shore of the 14th Regiment with his wife and four daughters aged between nine months and eighteen years. Despite some drunkenness among the crew, which resulted in two seamen being disciplined, the voyage was reasonably uneventful.

The Isles of Scilly were passed on the morning of Sunday, 9th October and as *Clarendon* sailed on up Channel the weather became blustery and unsettled. By Monday night gale force winds were battering the back of the Wight, and the Coastguard were at their stations. Just before six o'clock, in the dim light of early morning, the watchers on the cliffs above Blackgang saw a ship running before the howling wind, heading straight into the shore. The firing of the warning maroons brought people running from their homes down to the beach to stand and gaze in awestruck dismay as *Clarendon* drove into the bay.

Once again we meet that too often repeated scenario of a ship carried on to a lee shore by wind and tide, her fate made more certain by being 'embayed', or driven into a bay beyond whose headlands she could not beat against the wind. In sailing-ship days it was one of the commonest causes of loss, often caused by insufficient navigational information. A ship coming up from the west, as was the *Clarendon* in bad weather, making for Southampton or Portsmouth, would often sail the long way around the Wight rather than risk the tricky Needles Channel, a longer but safer route so long as a course was kept well off the Island's South coast. But in the inky blackness of a stormy October night a captain unable to fix his position or accurately calculate leeway and tidal set could find himself in trouble. For *Clarendon* a light, almost anywhere, would have saved her, but there was no light and *Clarendon* was lost.

Clarendon hit the beach, hardly twice her own length from the shore where, according to the survivors, those on board could see their would-be rescuers waiting, helpless to reach them against the fury of the storm. The stranded vessel barely lasted for five minutes. The huge waves threw her broadside on to the beach, rolling her over on to her side. The yards, like massive javelins pierced the sand, the masts snapped or tore themselves out of the ship. With her hull so disastrously weakened the *Clarendon* could not hold her heavy cargo of casks and boxes. She literally exploded under the enormous stress and within a few moments was simply a mass of shattered timbers littering sea and shore. Somewhere among it all were her passengers and crew, but of the twenty eight *Clarendon* carried with her on to the beach only three were alive. They were all crew members – James Harris, the second mate, and two seamen, William Byrne and John Thompson.

Byrne's testimony at the subsequent inquest illustrates very well the uncertainties of navigation almost until present times. Men had been voyaging round the oceans of the world since the 15th century, but the greatest hazards were not to be found upon the open seas, so much as near the end of a voyage, when failure to identify his landfall with certainty, due to bad weather or poor visibility could put the seamen in dire peril. That is precisely what happened to the *Clarendon*.

Byrne, an experienced seaman told the inquest ' . . . I am certain it was Scilly we made on Sunday. I knew it by the light-house. We continued in sight of land all night. I saw the Lizard light; we had two lights in one. I lost sight of them about 10 p.m. and saw no land to be certain after. About midnight I saw a light which appeared to be a revolving one, but it might possibly have been the motion of the ship. I did not know whether it was the Portland or the Needles light . . .'.

The captain was drowned and unable to defend his navigation, but if he thought the same as Byrne, then to fix his position he had to choose one of two lighthouses over fifty miles apart, a degree of uncertainty which should have made him proceed with extreme caution.

Byrne also said that by two o'clock in the morning he knew the land he could see to leeward to be the Isle of Wight. But did the ship's officers? More than two hours passed before the danger to *Clarendon* was fully recognised and it was not the fury of the tempest that destroyed her, but the folly of those two wasted hours.

John Thompson, the other surviving seaman, in his evidence confirmed that a light was sighted at about midnight on Monday October 10th. He said Sherlock, another seaman, told him it was the Portland light and he guessed it to be about ten leagues to leeward, a ridiculous estimate for an experienced sailor, to make. Thompson was at the helm and perhaps twenty five feet above the water at the most. Ten leagues are thirty miles and to see a light at that distance he would require both a very fine clear night, and either himself, or the light, to be almost five hundred feet up in the air. To see the Portland light

39

from his elevation he could not be more than about eighteen miles away and he would still need a clear cloudless night and not the rain soaked murk he was peering through. He might have been a competent helmsman but he was a rotten judge of distance at sea. Were any of the ship's officers any better? John Thompson put the wind at WSW, almost straight on shore. He was steering ESE, a converging course with the Island coast even without allowing for a strong leeward drift to worsen the situation. Given time and a long shore line, *Clarendon* was doomed, and she had enough of both.

The only surviving officer, James Harris, second mate, added little new. He was ill and in his bunk until 5.30 on Tuesday morning, he said, and did not go on deck until the ship was about a mile off shore. Harris did not know where they were. No one asked why the second mate, so vital a link in the chain of command, was allowed to lie in his bunk until the ship was almost ashore. Harris did however describe the fight to sail the ship out of the little bay. '. . . The ship was under double (reefed) main (lower) topsail, everything clewed. We set the fore (lower) topsail, foresail, fore and main (upper) topsails, trysails and spanker, and stood on dragging our bulwarks under water, but could not weather the point . . .'

Then Harris related how he was swept off the deck into the water, closely followed by the long boat which landed upsidedown on top of him. His instant reaction was to grab hold of the boat and, with it covering him, the waves flung him on the beach. Waiting there was John Wheeler a man of courage whose family name is respected still on the Isle of Wight. Wheeler saw Harris hanging on to the long boat, as it was swept on the beach and without the slightest hesitation dashed into the surf to get him as he floundered in the water, assailed from every side by wreckage. It was a difficult and dangerous endeavour but Wheeler saved him.

It was not the first time John Wheeler had entered the sea that wild night. John Thompson had actually jumped from the *Clarendon* into the boiling surf and within seconds was rolled on to the beach by the heavy breakers. Wheeler was one of three or four men who at once ran down the beach into the water, and grabbing hold of Thompson dragged him up the shore to safety. Thompson's relief at being snatched from the sea by Wheeler must have been matched only by his surprise. Both at one time had been shipmates aboard the Earl of Yarborough's yacht *Falcon*. While employed on *Falcon*, John

Thompson, a non swimmer, had fallen overboard and it was Wheeler who jumped after him; holding him up until a boat was lowered. It is not often a man's life is twice saved by the same person in similar circumstances.

William Byrne had also saved himself by leaping off the stranded hull before she broke up. He reasoned that if he could avoid being smashed to a pulp by wreckage he would only have the sea to contend with. Strangely, his arrival on the beach was un-noticed for some time, and he had the disquieting experience of sitting alone, safely ashore and watching his ship break apart in front of him. The inquest jury returned a verdict on the dead of accidentally drowned. A convenient enough reponse, but perhaps 'carelessly drowned' would have been more accurate.

Apart from the inquest proceedings all contemporary reports dwell morbidly on the aftermath of the wreck. One eyewitness wrote:

'That day I was scrambling about the beach in a sort of listless manner' (at a shipwreck?) 'when I was suddenly aroused by see a group of people standing around the dead body of a female. Among the by-standers were several women who looked at the body with stolid indifference. One of these asserted it was that of a soldiers wife. 'And if it was', I asked, 'what then?' Is it not the body of a woman like yourselves?'

In short I was so disgusted with their apathy, and want of feeling, that I remonstrated with them in anything but complementary terms.

However the writer spoils his holier than thou high mindedness by describing in such detail her fine features, her lovely and well formed limbs that the whole borders on the morally obscene.

But, to give credit where it is due the reporter, together with a Mr Charles Day of Ventnor and two other men, carried the body to a nearby hut on a stretcher made up from sugar cask staves. There John Spary, the postmaster at Ventnor, covered the dead woman with a mat and a piece of sail from the wreck. One by one the other battered bodies of the dead were washed ashore and in turn were taken up to the hut or a boathouse to await disposal. Then came the harrowing job of identifying the dead. Mr. Jacobs of Chale Abbey Farm, undertook the task of shepherding Byrne and Harris from body to body, lifting the covers from each in turn, waiting as the two men struggled to put a name to a battered and disfigured corpse. 'Yes, that's one of the girls –

41

she was singing away so last night – that's Mr. Shore's daughter – I don't know her name. Oh dear sir, this time yesterday none of us thought of this. That's one of Mr. Shore's – it's not Miss Pemberton.'

Mentioned from time to time throughout this book are the activities of so called wreckers. They were people who descended on every wreck – almost, it seems, with an uncanny premonition of the event. Their usual behaviour was to lay their hands on to anything they could carry, and if it was too big or heavy for one man then another would help, for a share of the profits. The business was as old as seafaring itself and totally illegal. Leaving aside such morally dubious privileges as 'right of wreck' claimed by local lords of the manor and Island governors it was simply theft on a grand scale, though often the presence of would-be wreckers provided manpower for launching lifeboats.

At the wreck of the *Clarendon* a very large crowd was gathered, but on this occasion there was no plundering. The local landowners Lord Yarborough and his son, the Honourable Mr Pelham, were there that morning and throughout the day. Rounding-up every one in sight they organised beach parties collecting the trunks and other personal possessions of the dead. Other parties carried the piles of remnants to various boathouses and huts in the locality, so that they could be claimed by next of kin. One reporter wrote: 'Almost everyone lent a hand to good purpose. The old wrecking feeling was awed, we hope for ever. On our conscience we do not think that one crown's worth of property was stolen during the day. Relics were taken but they were valuable only as memorials of the wreck or as emblems of superstition.'

It might be thought that over the succeeding years our reporter, in retrospect, could have become a little disillusioned. Perhaps on that day in 1835 the Lord Yarborough's eyes were a wee bit sharper than certain others approved.

Victor Emmanuel 1861

Most-real life stories of ships leave an impression of complete accord and understanding between the captain and his officers and crew. Every man on a merchant ship desired a fast, trouble free passage which depended on maximum co-operation and everybody on board knew also that ultimately their own safety depended on teamwork. Disagreements were bound to arise but in the main were resolved without an overt display of force. Bucko mates and evil captains flogging the crew round the ship to impose their overbearing authority belong more to the realms of fiction, for any shipmaster who tried to impose a regime of fear soon found himself able to recruit only the dregs of the dockside for a crew.

However, human nature being what it is, captains sometimes did disagree with their subordinate officers and refuse to listen to advice. But determination is one thing, unreasonable obstinacy is another, and can have disastrous results at sea as Captain Charles Box found out to his cost.

On Wednesday, January 30th 1861, the barque *Victor Emmanuel* of some 620 tons, was lost in a thick fog. That she was off the Isle of Wight was known, but where? Earlier that day at about 3 o'clock in the afternoon and some ten miles out from land, the vessel had sailed past Portland Bill. A course east by south, (101¼ degrees), was set, but from then on the coast had been hidden by the swirling mist and checks on the ship's position were impossible. Although the wind was moderate a fierce ground swell was sweeping into the land and the *Victor Emmanuel* rolled uncomfortably in the beam seas. At about eight o'clock that evening the boatswain Robert Burns, who was standing watch, could see dead ahead the loom of a light which he reasoned to be St. Catherine's lighthouse on the southernmost tip of the Isle of Wight. He decided at once to inform the captain who was in his cabin.

Captain Box was about fifty years old and newly appointed to *Victor Emmanuel*, but he was familiar with the trade in which the ship normally engaged, the conveyance of agricultural produce from Egypt to Britain. On this occasion she was on passage from Alexandria to London with a cargo of beans, barley, wool and flax. It had lately become a prosperous trade. The repeal of the corn laws in 1846 had opened Britain to foreign competition, to the detriment of British farming interests but the benefit of the poorer part of the population. Cheap corn from Russia and America had flooded in, but the Crimean War in 1856 and the American Civil War in 1861 virtually eliminated those two countries as suppliers for some years. However, Egypt, at one time the granary of the Roman Empire, was ready to fill the gap and *Victor Emmanuel*, with holds full of Egyptian produce was on her way home, either to feed the poor or to destroy British farms, depending on the view you took of what was then a very emotive issue.

We don't know whether, in the voyage now nearing its end, the crew of *Victor Emmanuel* had come to like or dislike their new captain, but we begin to get an idea of his relations with them by his reception of the boatswain's report of the light. It was a scornful 'impossible'. This attitude was based on the course of east by south he had set from Portland which would take the ship well clear of land. A more prudent seaman would have asked himself whether the course ordered was also the course made good. However, at the insistence of the boatswain Captain Box went up on deck and, glancing in the direction Burns pointed, declared he could see nothing. Somewhat put out by this Robert Burns walked away from his captain and went forward, but obviously very concerned for the barque's safety he returned and again pointed out the light. At last Captain Box agreed that he too could see a light, but he could not say if it was showing from land or a ship, but whatever it was he was certain it was not St. Catherine's and that was that.

Nevertheless Box ordered the course to be changed to east south east, a course which would have taken the ship further out to sea and saved her, had he not, after only ten minutes, brought the *Victor Emmanuel* back to her original course and instructed George White, the helmsman, not to alter it without his direct orders. At the same time he also warned Robert Burns to make no more false reports about lights.

After about twenty minutes the light was again seen and its bearing from the ship had not altered, a sign which Box, who was still on deck, could not ignore. He ordered the barque to be hove-to and soundings taken. There was but three and a half fathoms of water and at that instant the *Victor Emmanuel* struck bottom. She was aground in Chale Bay, barely two or three miles from St Catherine's point.

As the leadsman called the sounding, George White at the wheel prepared to put the helm down to bring the barque's head around to fill the sails in order to get steerage way on the ship, the usual practice as soon as a sounding was complete. But Captain Box instantly ordered him to stay. So with little rudder control and the sails barely drawing, every succeeding roller drove the *Victor Emmanuel* towards the beach. That last order was fatal. The ship's head swung around down wind and she drove onto the shore.

Could the vessel yet be saved? The boatswain thought so, for he ordered the anchors to be let go. High tide was two hours away and if the ship could be held from driving further ashore perhaps she could be pulled free. But yet again Captain Charles Box countermanded the order. In so doing he sealed the fate of the ship.

The recognised signal for assistance at that period was the burning of so called 'blue lights'. These were a pyrotechnic device with an intense blue flame that could be seen, in reasonably good visibility, for a considerable distance. But although such lights were displayed for nearly an hour, so thick was the fog they were unobserved. By now the ship lay aground, broadside on to the swell and violently rolled from side to side, so much so that the crew were unable to fire any of the guns in a further bid to attract attention. With the ship now showing signs of breaking up it was time to get off.

By nine o'clock the ship's three boats were ready to be launched. First to be lowered was the gig, a long slender boat totally unsuited to such steep seas. Uncontrollable, it swung against the ship's side and simply smashed to bits. Luckily nobody was in it. Next was the long boat, and that too met the same fate, but this time the third mate, William Kane, who was trying to board it, was thrown into the water and drowned.

The immense ground swell was causing all the trouble, but if a boat could be pulled clear of the ship it would be reasonably safe. The mate and seven other men stood ready and, judging the moment to a nicety, dropped the third boat, the jolly boat, into the water. Every man knew what he had to do. It was into the boat, grab an oar and pull for dear life. Pull they did, desperately with all their strength, out to sea away from the wreck and the menacing shore. Later that night they were seen and picked up by a French ship, the *Etoile*, and taken on to Southampton, although they did not arrive at that port until early morning on Saturday, February 2nd. The eight lucky seamen then proceeded to London by train where they presented themselves at the offices of Messrs. Joyce, the charterers of the *Victor Emmanuel*, to claim their wages.

For some reason the boatswain did not know of the successful launch of the jolly boat which he thought was still in its davits when the ship broke up. Was it an example of eight men being company but nine a crowd?

The *Victor Emmanuel* started to go to pieces between half past nine and ten o'clock that night. John Constant, a Greek seaman, succeeded in clambering on to a hatch cover, but never reached the shore and his battered body was later recovered from the sea. William Easter, a deck hand, ran forward and climbed out onto the jib-boom calling for George White to join him. Before White could make up his mind whether to do so or not, the decision was made for him. The fore part of the ship collapsed and Easter disappeared. He also was later found dead, washed up on the beach.

Barely had he recovered from the shock of seeing William Easter vanish in a turmoil of splintering timbers than George White himself was hurled into the surf. But suddenly he was in shallow water being flung in all directions by the breaking waves. Then for one short moment he found himself laying on the shore, uncovered by the water and beside him a piece of iron sticking up out of the sand. Grimly hanging on to the iron bar he sorted out, in his mind, in which direction lay dry land and survival. This he did while all the time he was battered by the pounding waves. Then choosing exactly the right moment between breakers he tottered up the beach as fast as his trembling legs would take him.

Once safely on the beach George White was relieved and overjoyed to find three other survivors from the wreck. Creeping along the foot of the cliffs they found a boathouse where they rested for a couple of hours and, their composure recovered, then set off in search of help. Remember, the four men had just crawled out of the bitterly cold sea and were clambering around the cliffs in wringing wet clothes in the middle of a winter's night. Seeing a light, the little group of survivors hastened towards it. Finding it to be a house, George White and his shipmates hammered on the door, but the occupier had some very firm ideas about people who knocked him up in the dead of night, especially four men looking like rough desperadoes. He refused to let them into the house and would not believe their story. Shipwreck? What shipwreck? He knew of none. However, the four, eventually, did get directions to the Atherfield Coastguard Station where officers of the Shipwrecked Mariners Society made them welcome and dried them out.

On Friday evening, February 1st, the Isle of Wight Coroner, Mr. F. Blake, held an inquest at the Clarendon Hotel, Chale, on four seamen whose bodies were recovered from the *Victor Emmanuel*. The Clarendon Hotel itself was so named because of that other shipwreck in Chale Bay some twenty five years earlier.

The wreck of the *Clarendon* caused a great outcry for improved rescue services on the 'back of the Wight', public emotion being especially aroused by the loss of children in that wreck. A direct result of the public clamour following the loss of the *Clarendon* was the erection of St. Catherine's lighthouse, now known to mariners the world over as one of the most prominent navigation aids on the English south coast. Its light was first displayed on the night of March 1st 1840. So when the *Victor Emanuel* sailed along on that fatal night the light had warned mariners of danger for twentyone years. It was clearly marked on charts. But for all the notice that Captain Box took of it, it might just as well not been there.

The four dead men at the focus of the inquest were William Kane, third officer; John Pappoo, the ship's cook described as an African; William Easter and the Greek seaman John Constant. The miserable story of the wrecking and the events that led up to it were recounted by Robert Burns, George White and the two other un-named survivors. A verdict of accidental death was recorded. A week later the body of Captain Charles Box was washed ashore at Ventnor and identified by a stocking marked with his name. Although the boatswain, Robert Burns, one of the four men to reach the shore, said that he saw Captain Box washed overboard, another account has it that the captain was lost because when the ship broke up he was in his cabin trying to secure £60 in gold. If so he continues to the end to show the lack of judgement and common sense that cost him his own life, the lives of six crewmen, and his ship.

The captain's disastrous obstinacy was a mystery not unravelled by the inquest which was itself shrouded in some mystery. The ship was wrecked on the evening of Wednesday, January 30th and the inquest held only forty-eight hours later on the evening of Friday, February 1st, an uncommon haste for which no explanation is to be found. It is usual to gather information from every source, yet it must be assumed that everybody connected with the proceedings believed, or was prepared to accept, that only the four who came safely ashore were alive. The fact that eight more men had survived was unknown at the inquest. They didn't turn up until the following morning and, without a moment's delay, rushed off to London. The mate and his seven companions would have already vanished into thin air before the Coroner, would know of their rescue and arrival at Southampton. Also unknown at the inquest was the fate or whereabouts of the captain and two other crewmen, the steward and fifteen years old John Randall from Jersey. The bodies of those two were never found. But no matter how unsatisfactory it might be, the inquest holds for us all we now shall ever know of the loss of the *Victor Emmanuel*.

Meanwhile the cargo that was then being washed out of the shattered vessel covered the beach with beans and barley. People from all over the Isle of Wight came to cart it away and a considerable traffic went on for a couple of weeks. Of no use for anything else, it was very good for pigs, and it was free.

It still remains to ask the questions the inquest did not ask. Why should a ship with plenty of sea room and professed to be on a course that would take her well clear of land nevertheless go ashore? A course of east by south ($101^{1}/_{4}$ degrees) sailed from a position ten miles out from Portland Bill will bring a ship off St. Catherine's Point at a distance of thirty-five miles out to sea, well clear of land and with a good margin of safety for errors. This assumes that the boatswain was right about the distance off Portland, and that the track sailed really was $101^{1}/_{4}$ degrees.

The wind is described as moderate by Burns who claimed that the *Victor Emmanuel* was sailing in an eight knot wind. This cannot be correct if the times given for passing Portland and arriving at Chale are correct. If the times are right then the barque needed to sail at least at ten knots over the whole five hours to travel the fifty odd miles in the time. By implication the wind was much stronger than the boatswain estimated, although ten knots does seem a little high for a ship that had been at sea for some time. The groundswell that figures so prominently would have been raised by high winds blowing for a long time. It begins to appear likely that the *Victor Emmanuel* had endured some stormy weather on her way up channel, and although the wind had decreased it was still much higher than Robert Burns had estimated.

If we suppose that the ship was more like five miles out when she passed Portland Bill, a different picture emerges. A glance at the tidal stream atlas will show that before local high water a powerful tidal stream moves up channel, the landward edge closely following the contours of the south coast. Where headlands intrude into the stream the water flow speeds up, one reason for the famous Portland Race and lesser ones round headlands such as St. Catherine's. Passing the restriction of St Aldhelm's Head the flow sets strongly into Poole Bay where it divides into two separate streams, one flowing north east into the Solent through the Needles channel, the other south east down the back of the Wight.

With this in mind the events leading up to the loss of the *Victor Emmanuel* can be reconstructed with some degree of certainty. After a rough trip across the Bay of Biscay and into the English Channel the barque made landfall at Portland Bill, but in the poor visibility was much closer inshore than estimated. Added to the murky conditions was the onset of nightfall, both together preventing an accurate fix of the ship's position. A course of east by south, (101¼ degrees), was set, and in theory should have taken the ship clear of the Isle of Wight, but because the vessel was further into the land than thought, the influence of the tidal stream sweeping into Poole Bay was considerable.

So with a stronger onshore wind and more leeway than may have been allowed for, the landward set of the groundswell, the effect of the tidal flow, and a wrong assumption of her original position the ship was put into a position of danger.

And yet, even then, if Captain Box had been a less obstinate man and had listened to his boatswain, the *Victor Emmanuel* could have sailed on her way, unscathed, with nothing worse than a mild fright.

Cedarine 1862

Shipwrecks are usually sad affairs with tales of the loss of fine ships and better men, but in many disasters can be found elements of light relief, and in a few, the making of a Will Hay farce. The events that followed the rescue of all on board the *Cedarine*, in retrospect at least, must fall into the last category. Although it is to be doubted if those on board at the time thought it so, contemporary reports dismissed the wreck as rather uninteresting. That meant that there was no harrowing drowning stories to relate, for in an age when wrecks were all too common any not accompanied by loss of life attracted little attention. So in highly disapproving manner the reports concentrated solely on the activities of the survivors ashore. But for them there would be no story.

The *Cedarine* was a rather small, newly built vessel, barque rigged and given a contemporary measurment of 308 tons. According to some reports her name was bestowed on her because she was almost entirely constructed of cedar wood, but that seems a little unlikely. She was commanded by Captain Dill and had a crew of thirteen. In addition she carried six women and eighteen children, the families of three surgeons (Beck, King and Roberts), an overseer named Young and three warders who were in charge of 191 convicts. Altogether a total of 235 souls.

The convicts were men who had been sentenced to short term transportation to Bermuda; some were coming home to be freed, having served their time, and the others were good conduct ticket-of-leave men.

The *Cedarine* sailed from Bermuda on March 15th, 1862, and was battered by stormy weather throughout the homeward voyage. On her entering the Channel the wind was still strong, coming from the south west accompanied by periods of very poor visibility. Suddenly, just before 2 p.m. on Wednesday April 2nd, through a short break in the fog, land was seen over the bow and the helm was put down immediately to bring the ship round. Unfortunately the sails did not fill and she ran aground midway between the Ship Ledge and Brighstone Grange, about 200 yards out from the beach. Every successive wave of the pounding sea drove the barque in until she was only fifty-yards off the shore. Luckily, for the hapless people on her, the

50

ground over which she was driven was smooth and sandy, without exposed rocks to rip the bottom out, as so often was the case in shipwrecks along that coast.

The plight of the *Cedarine* was immediately discovered and Mr Cutijar, commanding officer of the Atherfield coastguard station raised the alarm for the Brighstone lifeboat to be prepared and launched. He then hurried to the beach where he found the Rector of Brook, the Reverend John Pellow Gaze already organising means of rescue.

The lifeboat being ready and the crew assembled John Brooke of Brighstone Grange, using his own horses, superintended the moving of the boat from the boathouse down to the beach where, at no little risk to themselves in the heavy surf, the gathering crowd of onlookers assisted its launch.

While all this activity was taking place on the beach, a hawser, made fast at one end to the jib-boom of the *Cedarine*, had been successfully floated ashore and using this as a lifeline some of the convicts began making their way to safety. Members of the Coastguard entered the sea with ropes to drag out those whose strength was failing. Coastguard Kendereen in particular distinguished himself by his tireless and daring exertions at this task.

The lifeboat now appeared at the scene and on her first trip to the wreck took off the women and children. This boat was provided and paid for by public subscription and placed on station at Brook Chine in 1860. She proved herself an admirable craft in the wild tempestuous seas, ably repaying her donors and the complete confidence of her gallant crew. Seven times more the lifeboat returned to the ship and brought ashore all the remaining people on board, rescuing a total of 128 souls. Of the 235 persons originally on board not one was lost, a text book example of an efficient, speedy, well organised rescue operation to match any on record. However, the events that followed, once all the men were on dry land were a little more chaotic.

News of nearly 200 convicts roaming ashore was obviously alarming for the local population and messengers were despatched without delay to Parkhurst Barracks for military aid, and to Portsmouth for a steamboat, though what purpose that was to serve is not clear. If it was to prevent an escape by sea it would have been rather pointless since nearly all of the convicts were heading for eventual release and it is to be doubted if any would willingly have re-entered that wild sea having once escaped from it.

Throughout the remaining hours of that Wednesday the public generally could get little accurate news, and as the rain fell in torrents few people outside the immediate area were inclined to venture forth. Amidst the uncertainty '. . . Rumour who doth double, like voice and echo . . .' was rife. At one time it was reported that above one hundred convicts were drowned before they could be brought up on deck. Speculation was also entered into as to whether the Government would be liable to actions for damages brought by wives or others '. . . who could show a pecuniary interest in a dead convict, though they would repudiate a live one, as in railway slaughters . . .'

Although correct, the rumour that all were saved, mostly by the lifeboat, was soon discounted by those who insisted that the lifeboat had nothing to do with it at all. The greatest alarm was caused by a piece of bloodthirsty reporting that had all the convicts safe, but that they had turned on their keepers and their families and killed every one of them.

Thursday morning at last dawned and news of the strange happenings ashore began to leak out. As soon as the request for aid was received a military detachment was despatched from Parkhurst, but it took several hours for them to reach Brighstone from Newport on foot. Before the soldiers arrived at the scene the convicts, ignoring the handful of guards, made off to Brighstone village, seemingly none the worse for their experiences in the dangerous sea. To men denied them for so long, the good things of life were calling too loudly to be resisted. In addition to having some money the convicts were reported to have stolen stores from the *Cedarine* including piles of blankets, although those items might have been provided to the survivors as they came ashore. Be that as it may, nearly two hundred men invaded the two public houses at Brighstone, the Five Bells and the New Inn (now called Three Bishops). Those without money bartered the blankets and stores. All that, together no doubt with a fair sprinkling of threatening behaviour, soon had the pubs running dry.

The effect of abundant alcohol on men straight from a regimented penal colony and a confined sea voyage can well be imagined. The least troublesome were those lying around the roads in a stupor; it was the disturbances caused by those convicts who could still stand up that came in for criticism. As these men progressively became more and more drunk they became increasingly quarrelsome. Fights broke out, spreading from group to group, until Brighstone resembled a battle-field. The narrow roads and lanes were littered with bodies of the insensible and incapable.

As Victorian society, publicly at least, had a strongly moral out-look, such scenes of drunken debauchery were an anathema to it and were strongly condemned in contemporary accounts, but in an at-tempt to redress the balance much was made of the conduct of many prisoners who, at their own request, were allowed to march unat-tended by guards from Brighstone to Parkhurst Barracks. After many privations in Bermuda the brawlers in Brighstone, wreck and storms forgotten, were obviously enjoying themselves, but the arrival of the military quickly put a stop to that. Carts and wagons were obtained, convicts rounded up, a strong escort mounted and off to Parkhurst Barracks they all went and that was the end of that. Or not quite.

The columns of local newspapers went on debating whether any of the convicts had made a bid to escape, though assuring readers that none had succeeded.

And one even more outrageous rumour cropped up. It was sug-gested that some of the soldiers sent to protect the populace from the dangerous criminals had found that strong drink was to be had for the asking, had broached a cask or two and had joined the convicts in the punch-up. So perhaps it was not only uniforms of prison grey that lay insensible in the bottom of the carts as they rumbled back across the island.

Ellen Horsfall and Lotus 1862

Since the great storm of October 1826, during which the *Clarendon* was wrecked at Blackgang Chine, nobody could recollect another gale of equal severity until that of Saturday, October 18th 1862. That day saw the start of a storm which long remained in the public memory. Fearful squalls, veering from south east to south west, accompanied by heavy rain, battered the Isle of Wight. The rain was so unremitting that ships sheltering off the Mother Bank in the Solent were invisible from the Island shore, and men-of-war anchored at Spithead sent down their topmasts for security.

Worst affected was the south west coast of the Wight; the stretch from the Needles to St. Catherines known to all locals as 'the back'. All along that coast the coastguards and fishermen stood by, but so wild was the wind and sea there would have been but little hope for launching a boat to attempt a rescue. As Saturday night slowly passed and Sunday morning dawned the wind shifted to the west north west and lessened a little in strength. The weather cleared to give a bright day; so welcome after the dreadful night before.

Sunday October 19th passed with little improvement in weather conditions, but without incident, and as night fell the lookouts on the cliffs dispersed. They included men styled as 'wreckers' but that meant nothing more sinister than men waiting in the hope of picking up, albeit illegally, anything washed ashore from a wreck. They sometimes also saved a poor sailor from the surf, or helped to launch a lifeboat, so were not altogether without merit.

At about 9 o'clock that evening the barque *Ellen Horsfall* ran aground near Grange Chine. Like the *Victor Emmanuel* she too was engaged in the business of importing foodstuffs from Egypt into Britain. Only a small vessel of 293 tons, her cargo seems to have consisted entirely of beans. The weather was still very wild and the night so dark that *Ellen Horsfall*'s arrival on the beach was unseen.

It is easy to picture the ship, pounded by the heavy surf and her boats smashed, slowly breaking up and every hope gone of rescue for her crew. At another time and place all would have been lost. But not at Grange Chine that night. In a desperate bid to do something positive and not just wait to drown, a seaman, with a rope tied about his waist, leapt into the ranging sea and managed to swim ashore. By

54

good fortune the waves swept him around a large rock, to which without more ado he made fast his life line, and then went off in search of assistance. He remains an unknown hero for nobody bothered to ask him his name. Finding a cottage he roused the sleeping inmates who in turn awoke their neighbours, all fishermen, who hurried to the beach where a successful rescue was carried out. All on the *Ellen Horsfall* were lifted off before the barque went to pieces. Exactly how the rescue was mounted and performed contemporary accounts do not say, but it seems probable that the fishermen rowed out to the wreck. The ship's master, Captain Mabey, and his wife and small child were among those saved.

Mr. Mowbray, a farmer, was waiting for them on the cliff and without delay carted off the wet and exhausted survivors to Thorn- cross Farm where they rested all the next day. On Tuesday, October 21st a coach was provided to take them to Cowes where they boarded the steamer *Emerald* for Southampton to catch the train to London. So for them all ended well, but the *Ellen Horsfall* was not the only shipwreck on the back of the Wight that Sunday.

The ship *Lotus*, 326 tons, inward bound from Demerara to London, laden with rum and sugar was working her way up Channel, with St. Catherine's light ahead, fine on her lee bow at 10 p.m. It was then found impossible to weather St. Catherine's Point. *Lotus* was standing too close to the land; a couple of miles further out and she would have cleared the headland without danger.

She was wrecked at Blackgang, but reports differ widely as to when. One says that the ship was lost at about 10.30 p.m. on Sunday night with the wind south by east. However, in the same newspaper another account 'from our Ventnor Correspondent' carefully analyses the fundamental causes of the disaster but times it as five o'clock on the following morning. The second report also differs in the direction of the wind which it gives as north west. Because of the care 'our Ventnor Correspondent' displays in marshalling the facts his report is more likely to be accurate, and is the preferred version so far as this writer is concerned.

He was most emphatic that the *Lotus* had been disabled in the storms over the weekend because she was old and unseaworthy and the very reasons, he argued, why she fell to pieces so quickly after striking. With the tide on the ebb and the wind from the north west, the *Lotus* should have had no difficulty in keeping off the land.

Everything went to prove she was already crippled.

Whatever reasons, her end was swift. In a matter of minutes she fell apart, giving her crew, under Captain William McNicol, no time to save themselves. Including the one passenger, a Mr E. Murry of Dublin, there were fourteen men on the ship and only two, John Gold and James Anderson, survived. They also went to Southampton by the *Emerald* on Tuesday, October 21st. Their lost shipmates (McNiel, Watt, Henderson, Montgomery, Ferguson, Paterson, Durrock, Lamb, Kelly, Matthews and Dunbin) found their last haven in Chale churchyard, piloted there, as the report says, 'in a praiseworthy manner' by the Reverend Mr Theobald.

If any cargo could cause trouble then rum, most assuredly, would do just that. A considerable number of casks were washed in, but although most were smashed on the rocks, many were not. Accusations of drunkenness were levelled at the rescue services, and stories of men too drunk to save life were rife. Public feelings ran high.

To investigate the situation for himself our friend the Ventnor Correspondent visited Rocken End Point where the *Lotus* came ashore. He could hardly descend the narrow path to the beach because of crowds of people, 'the wreckers', coming up the pathway laden with timber. Apart from the scene of devastation that met his eyes when he at last gained the beach, his attention was drawn to the piles of undamaged rum barrels. He took particular notice of a cask which had been opened and around which was a small crowd of people. Some were filling bottles, some had buckets which they filled to the brim and tried to carry away without spilling any of the precious contents; all the while slipping and sliding on the stones. There were some who, not knowing what to expect had arrived unprepared, without containers of any sort except themselves. Not to be denied the same pleasures as their neighbours they were dipping out the rum with cupped hands and quaffing the liquid on the spot. If the newspaper correspondent had trouble in going down the path, many others would have worse problems going up!

It was the description of these scenes that provoked fierce criticism and the charges of drunkenness, with rival newspapers taking sides on the issue. The community was divided between these who were shocked at the alleged behaviour and those who hotly denied the truth of it. One reporter classed the purveyors of such scurrilous rumours as 'land sharks and Newport snobs' and 'worst of all . . . coal trimmers connected with a Southampton newspaper' (a bit hard on coal trimmers). The Ventnor man admitted that although he himself had not seen any, he had heard of several cases of drunkenness, but dismissed the complaints with the excuse that 'they were only youths and poor people'.

Unfortunately, the central issue, of whether men drowned because other men were drunk, was itself submerged under the flood of verbiage. It is noteworthy that more space was taken up with the accusations and denials of drunken behaviour than was given to the shipwreck itself. Perhaps sailors, like youths and the poor, merited but scant attention. Or was it that getting oneself drowned was, however regrettable, not such an affront to Victorian morals as getting drunk in public on someone else's rum?

Suavé Gardé ashore at Shanklin in 1866. A detail from a contemporary oil painting (Isle of Wight County Council)

Sauvé-Gardé 1866

Most of the ships which were wrecked by running aground at the back of the Wight stayed ashore once grounded, but some were salvaged to sail again. Among that fortunate company was the *Sauvé-Gardé*, a fine new French built and owned ship.

The salvage story spread over six months, but the various accounts do not fix exactly the date of her grounding. It can, however, be placed with reasonable confidence in the first week of February 1866.

Sauvé-Gardé sailed from London to Bordeaux, the return leg of the first voyage, in ballast. She would be loaded with stones and shingle, perhaps almost to her half load line to avoid sailing fully light which would have dangerously reduced her stability, and made her very crank. Nevertheless sometime around February 1st the 800 ton ship drove ashore head-on, striking the rocks near Luccombe Chine, Shanklin. Luckily the only material damage was a hole in the bow, and that obviously not excessively large. Once the extent of the injury was established salvage attempt was immediately decided upon and the Royal Dockyard at Portsmouth commissioned to carry out repairs to the hull.

As damage was confined to the bow it was a fairly simple job to build a watertight bulkhead upwards from the forward bilge to the deck above. Any water leaking past the temporary bulkhead could easily be handled by a steam pump. Having no cargo aboard made the job relatively simple and no doubt to lighten the ship a fairly substantial amount of the ballast would have been shovelled out to speed the work further. The bulkhead was in position by the end of February and final preparations for the refloating put in hand.

Those preparations would have included surveying the immediate area around the *Sauvé-Gardé* for possible underwater obstructions. Any rocks in the vicinity could then be shifted or blasted. It would also be necessary to ship steam driven pumps to control any un-expected water inflow when the ship refloated. As sailing ships at that date did not have their own source of steam it was usual for a tug to be made fast alongside and the steam feed lines piped into the tug's own system through valves and fittings already installed for that purpose. Some tugs carried a separate boiler that was only used for salvage work. Should it be impossible to get a steam tug close enough to the wreck then a portable boiler had to be lifted into the stranded ship. Study of the reports suggests the latter was the method used in this case.

Unfortunately things went wrong. A storm on March 1st shifted the now light ship and slammed her down on nearby, and until then unsuspected rocks which bilged her. While trying to free her the water poured in faster than it could be pumped out, and with no alternative action available, the pumps were stopped and the ship allowed to flood. With summer not too far away, and with it the expectation of fine weather, the *Sauvé-Garde* was thought safe enought there while her mortified salvors had another think.

The Dockyard contractors now suggested that a complete false deck be laid to close off the bilges from the rest of the ship, but the French owners refused to sanction the idea. It was not in any way an exceptional operation. Such decks, known as spar decks, were commonly used in salvage attempts, but the cost was daunting. Great quantities of timber were required and considerable numbers of skilled men employed without any guarantee of success.

The agent for the insurance underwriters, and the captain of the ship, who was in all probability also part owner, requested the Dockyard to cease all activities while the future of the ship was decided. Eventually they decided to abandon the salvage attempt and sell her for scrap.

The *Sauvé-Gardé*, a new vessel that had cost about £13,000 to build was disposed of at a public auction by Mr J. B. May for the trifling sum of £500, but the new owners had a scheme of their own. The purchasers of the ship, Messrs Morgan and Mr Alfred Shepard, having bought the vessel at scrap price, had every intention of salving her, but not at their cost. The £500 was all they would risk, and if the salvage attempt failed it would soon be recovered by the sale of the timber and fittings. The ship was handed over to a Mr Langdon of Ryde, a man, we must assume, fully experienced in marine salvage.

Mr. Langdon's brief was simple. If he saved the *Sauvé-Gardé* a quarter share of her value would be his, if he failed, nothing. To take the job on such terms Langdon must have had fewer doubts about a successful outcome than even the rather sharp trio Messrs Morgan, Morgan and Shepard. The writer of one report had kept his eye on the work carried out by Langdon and was immensely impressed, not the least by the considerable sums of money spent. Apart from the labour charges, mostly incurred in laying the once rejected spar deck, and the material costs of the deck itself, there was also the expense of 'filling her with empty casks, gutta-percha air bags, and other appliances to boot, besides hiring steam pumps, steam tugs and procuring every assistance from the shore' a very formidable list.

At high tide around midday on Tuesday August 28th, the *Sauvé-Gardé* floated off the rocks and, gently pulled by a tug, proceeded to sea for the first time in six months. But triumph soon turned to dismay when a steam pump stopped and the tide suddenly proved more powerful than the tug. Presented with the possibility of her sinking, the tide was allowed to sweep the ship on to the beach barely a mile away from her late resting place. The shore, although strewn with rubble, was without large rocks. For a while the *Sauvé-Gardé* was all but given up for lost once again, but the doughty Mr. Langdon rallied his troops, called for reinforcements, and renewed the fight.

Work was resumed on the morning of Thursday August 30th and this time three tugs were in attendance. Working together the trio slowly pulled the *Sauvé-Gardé* off the beach and headed for Cowes, arriving at Osborne Bay that evening. There she waited until the following morning while a repair berth was procured in the Medina River.

Satisfaction on the outcome of the enterprise was expressed in all quarters. A fine ship was saved, and an excellent profit made. The newspapers were most effusive in their admiration.

Wreckage of *Talé Bauré* at Sandown, 1866 as depicted in the *Illustrated London News* on March 31st that year

Talé Bauré 1866

Sandown Bay, to the holidaymaker sitting on the beach and curling his toes into the warm sand, must seem an idyllic place. The pleasant vision of the sparkling sea, moving gently with little wavelets that inaudibly break and run but a couple of feet up the strand, might delude the stranger into the belief it is always thus. How mistaken they would be.

On March 23rd 1866 heavy seas backed by gale force winds, were pounding the beach in the bay and everywhere along the coast rescue services were on the alert. Just before eight o'clock that evening three vessels entered the bay from the south west and it was soon obvious they were standing into danger and likely to become embayed. With the wind blowing straight into Sandown Bay the three ships, unable to clear the encircling land, would be driven onto the lee shore. As soon as the situation was evident, the Coastguards fired a number of signal rockets and lit 'port fires' to warn the ships of the impending danger. All three turned away seawards and two successfully cleared Culver point. The third vessel, being much closer to the shore, was unlucky, grounding almost immediately afterwards.

This unfortunate craft was the brig *Talé Bauré* of Sweden, not a large vessel, probably about 500 tons, carrying a crew of twelve seamen including the captain, named Scrogland. The *Talé Bauré* was laden with a mixed cargo that included salt, oranges and figs and was on passage up channel bound for Bergen to Norway. It was suggested the *Talé Bauré* was an old ship, although how old, we don't know, and that she was built of deal. Deal of course implies fir or pine and although frowned upon by British shipbuilders many thousands of ships must have been built by Baltic shipyards using such woods. The brig's age and timber were reason enough to account for her rapid and almost total disintegration after she struck.

In the heavy swell and pounding breakers the *Talé Bauré* rolled and pitched and the crew, in their efforts to lessen the violent motion, resorted to the usual remedies. First the foremast and then the main-mast were cut away to reduce the weight aloft and the stresses on the hull. This appeared to the gathering crowd of observers to steady the ship considerably, but without masts or sails the vessel was utterly at the mercy of wind, wave and the now flooding tide.

Meanwhile, intending to mount an immediate rescue the Coast-guards had dragged their rowing boat onto the beach, but because Mister Bunt, the chief boatman, had sent men up to the top of Culver Cliff, he found he was short of two men to make up his crew. The missing crew members were up on the cliff to watch the progress of the other two ships and report back if and when they had cleared the Culver headland. Assembled on the beach, amongst the inevitable crowd of onlookers, were some fishermen and Bunt directly asked this group for volunteers. 'But to their shame be it spoken, not one would come forward to assist in the attempt to save the lives of twelve fellow creaures' said a local report.

It must be remembered that the Coastguard's boat was not a lifeboat and although obviously well built to enable them to perform their normal duties, it lacked the qualities necessary for it to be taken into such a raging sea with confidence.

A reporter tells us that two or three 'gentlemen' offered their services but were refused, the chief boatman wanting men accustomed to heavy boat work. However, a coastguard arrived from the Shanklin station so without more ado the man, Richard Hurley, and a volunteer, John Hyde, were drafted into the boat. With a full crew the boat was launched and the first attempt was made by the Coastguard to reach the *Taté Bauré* but it was not successful. The boat was said to be very narrow and very crank, being liable to roll excessively and not at all fitted for such service. The crew on that fruitless journey were John Bunt, the chief boatman, Robert Hoar, John Moran, William Jennings (all Sandown station coastguards) and Richard Hurley (the Shanklin man), with John Hyde and John Raynor (two civilian volunteers).

Following this disappointing result it was realised a boat rescue would be impossible and a decision was made to fetch the rocket apparatus, held at St. Lawrence. Alfred and Austin Perkins were despatched in a horse drawn light van to collect the gear and instructed to return with utmost haste. Meanwhile the brig continued drifting towards the shore and the coastguards made another effort to reach the vessel by boat but again were defeated by the storm. Our reporter wrote: 'about 1.30 a.m. the ship began to part. The rending of her timbers and the cries and shrieks of the poor creatures on the wreck were now truly appalling and heart-rending'

With a slight moderation in the weather the coastguards made a third attempt and this time the boat reached the *Talé Bauré*. They plucked one man from the wreck and struggled through the heavy seas with him back to the beach. A fourth time the boat set out this time managing to lift off no fewer than six more seamen. Unfortunately, while returning to the shore three of her planks were stove in and the boat filled with water. It reached shore safely but any further foray to the wreck was now out of the question.

While the Coastguards were valiantly striving in their efforts, three fishermen, Silas Sothcott, Walter Main (or Mains) and Frank Hayden, in a small fishing boat belonging to Hayden, also set off in a rescue attempt. However, so hard did the three men have to pull on the oars, the thole pins holding the oars in place on the gunwale, were broken and a hasty return to the beach was necessary. After some hurried repairs the fishing boat put out again and reaching the brig took off four men and brought them safely back to land.

Once more the little fishing boat set out to the stricken brig, Samuel Calloway replacing an exhausted Walter Main and the sole remaining crew member was heaved into the boat and carried back to his shipmates waiting on the beach. When the rescued man was safely ashore and heads counted a great cheer was given by the watching crowd. Not always was an entire ship's crew saved; all too often it was just a case of collecting and burying the bodies.

The rocket rescue apparatus, despite some undoubted fast driving of the horse van, arrived too late to be used. A correspondent writing to the Isle of Wight Observer about the rescue urged the necessity of having a lifeboat stationed in the bay and further commented on the fact that 'There were not enough cork jackets for the men, nor were there any rockets with apparatus for carrying lines and the absence of these things was felt severely.'

Criticism was also voiced about the conduct of the watermen refusing to help man the Coastguard's boat. The watermen's excuse that the Coastguard's boat was unsuitable was looked on as a sad reflection of their courage. Suggestions were made that there was some very bad feeling between the fishermen and the Coastguard because the watermen had been prevented from carrying off wreckage from a vessel, the Sauvégardé then lying stranded at Shanklin. Accusations were also made that the watermen did not put out until the *Talé Bauré* was breaking up. One correspondent rather cynically wrote: 'But whether the cries of the poor creatures on the wreck or the thought of reward stimulated the heroism of the men I cannot say, but this I know, they received about £4–10s [£4.50p] each man from subscriptions raised on the spot, while the Coastguard who had been trying to reach the wreck all evening were looked on as having only done their duty and received nothing' The subscription list was started by Doctor Leeson, (after whom Leeson hill in Ventnor is named), and one hopes that the Coastguard crew had some well deserved recognition of their bravery, in addition to the gratitude of those saved from the wreck. In 1866 the yearly wage of chief boatman was only about £40, so the £4–10s presented to each fisherman was in the region of five weeks' pay for a Coastguard.

The survivors, having lost everything, were first taken to the Sandown Hotel to be given dry clothes and food and a bed for a few hours before being sent on their way. *Talé Bauré* finished up as matchwood in front of the Coastguard station, very close to the old Granite Fort, now the Sandown Zoo. Her remains were auctioned as scrap wood; 'such a total wreck as we have never before witnessed' said one description.

There was a sad postscript a few days later when Walter Main, one of the Sandown boatmen who went to the wreck appeared before the Ventnor magistrates charged with stealing a piece of rope from the brig but he was discharged with a caution. The defendant said he helped save the crew of the ship and if there was anything coming from the Royal Humane Society he would be glad to have it.

Underley, Hephzibah and Cassandra 1871

Underley was built in 1866 at Lancaster for the Liverpool and Lancashire Line, a fully rigged ship of 1,202 tons. Her beauty of line and form were admired by all and Captain Tidmarsh must have been well pleased with his command. But perhaps it would have been better for Underley if someone other than Tidmarsh had been giving the orders.

The ship sailed on Sunday September 24th from Gravesend, bound for Melbourne, Australia, but what normally would have been a long hard haul of about four months ended two days later. During the night of September 25th/26th a strong south-east gale, colloquially known as a 'Luccomber' to inhabitants of South Wight, swept in from the English Channel and struck the Underley close to land.

Why was she sneaking close in along the south coast of the Isle of Wight instead of standing well out, away from harm, away from that ever present possibility of finishing up on a lee shore? So many times we read of well-found ships, officered and crewed by experienced men, trapped on a lee shore without sea room to beat off to windward. And why they were so close inshore in the first place when their more obvious course was further out is a question just as often left unanswered. More ships have been lost on beaches than in deep water.

A little after three o'clock on the morning of Tuesday September 26th the Underley drove head foremost, 'all standing', onto the rocks near Dunnose Point between Luccombe and Bonchurch. It seems that the crew immediately following the grounding were preoccupied with furling the sails that they neglected to lay-out a kedge astern, as a consequence of which the vessel sheered round broadside onto the surf and firmly wedged herself in the rocks.

Although the Coastguard stations at Ventnor and Shanklin were aware of Underley's predicament they made for some reason no move towards the wreck until daylight. The local newspaper loyally remarked that 'as soon as it was light the men of the two stations lost no time in repairing to the scene of the disaster', but in fact they had waited three hours. Somewhere around half past six, the Coastguard boat was launched and, since it was an hour or more before high tide, they offered their assistance in getting Underley off the beach, but the offer was refused and when the tide began to ebb at about eight o'clock the Underley was soon high and dry.

Later that morning at ten o'clock, *Medusa* and *Grinder*, two government tugs from Portsmouth Dockyard, arrived on the scene but though both put their heaviest hawsers aboard the ship she would not budge. Since by then it was already two or three hours after high water this is not surprising. Something might have been achieved if the attempt had been made at the top of the tide, it seems likely she was badly holed and in any event at the commencement of a long voyage to Australia would be fully laden. It would have required a depth of water of eighteen or more feet to float her clear of the rocks. Without a very high tide and strong winds blowing on shore such a depth of water would not be realised so *Underley* was destined to remain on the rocks.

In the struggle to move the ship *Grinder* broke her best hawser and was forced to return to Portsmouth, supposedly to procure another, taking at the same time fifteen women passengers with her. *Grinder* was soon followed by *Medusa*: neither returned to the wreck. Although no report actually says so, we must assume that if the tug *Grinder* took off the women, the *Medusa* must have taken their men. The *Underley* was labelled an emigrant ship by the press, an appellation that invokes a vision of a vessel crammed with a couple of hundred passengers living in poor conditions. But the *Underley* carried only about thirty emigrants, probably better thought of as fifteen couples.

The departure of the two tugs was shortly followed by that of the Coastguard boat, but the rocket rescue team from the Ventnor station did remain and during Wednesday, September 27th, because of worsening conditions and concern for their safety, the rocket apparatus was used to take off the crew, all of whom were still on board. Unfortunately, the steward was washed overboard and drowned before he could be rescued. He was the only casualty suffered throughout the whole affair.

The crew of *Underley* was taken to East Dene, at Bonchurch, home of John Snowdon Henry, MP for South-east Lancashire. Captain Tidmarsh and Mr Spurgeon the pilot who was still aboard when the vessel stranded were lodged separately in the Commercial Inn, Ventnor.

Now it was obvious that the ship could not be re-floated and salvage of the cargo became the main concern. Taking advantage of a spell of fine weather the salvage agent put a large force of men on board on

The *Underley* shortly after grounding (Trustees Carisbrooke
Castle Museum)

October 1st. The weather deck of the ship was dry, even at high tide, and it was possible to use the donkey engine to raise the heaviest pieces of cargo from the hold. Since she was flooded throughout, divers had to do most of the work below, and for four weeks, almost nonstop, work went on at a frantic pace. Salvaged goods were first stowed on the deck and then at high tide transferred to lighters brought along-side for shipment to Portsmouth. The most valuable portions of the cargo, such as wines and spirits, were further sent on to London for auction.

Underley was wedged in the rocks in an almost upright position and that contributed in great measure to the rapid unloading of the goods. From the beach she had more the appearance of a ship at anchor than a wreck. Although steam driven pumps were taken on board with the intention of freeing the vessel of water when the merchandise, or as much as possible, had been removed, we can find no evidence of their use. The *Underley* was in all likelihood so badly holed that such pumps as were available would have been unequal to the task. Although the spell of fine weather facilitated salvage of the cargo it also encouraged unofficial removal and several persons were convicted of stealing from the wreck. Eventually the fine ship fell to pieces and all that remains are a few photographs to remind us of her sad end.

The enquiry into the loss of the *Underley* took place towards the end of October, 1871. The conclusion of the Inquiry Board bears out the point so often stressed in this book that particularly in the 19th century human failings of carelessness or ineptitude wrecked as many ships as wind and sea. And like so many such inquiries at the time it leaves many questions unanswered.

The summing up says: 'The Court is of the opinion that the *Underley* was wrecked through absence of due care on the part of Mr. Spurgeon the pilot, but the law does not relieve the master from his responsibility.' And it finds Captain Tidmarsh negligent 'in impro-perly leaving the ship in the sole charge of a person whose compulsory duties as defined by law had *ceased at Dungeness*', [my italics]. What on earth was Spurgeon doing on the Underley 100 miles from the place where he should have left her? Why was he still conducting the navigation of the ship? We are not told but Captain Tidmarsh did have his Master's Certificate suspended for three months, 'this meeting the justice of the case'.

That might have been the last the islanders heard of the *Underley*

The *Underley* with topmasts and yards gone. Note the lifting
gear rigged between fore and mainmasts to take off the cargo
(Trustees Carisbrooke Castle Museum)

Divers on board the *Underley* in 1871 (Illustration in the
London Graphic)

but for the story of the unfortunate Mr Joseph Marks. Nearly a month before the wreck of the *Underley* and certainly before Joseph Marks had even heard of her, he wrote a letter, published September 2nd 1871 to the *Ryde Ventilator*. Marks was a successful cutler and a gunsmith. He wrote:

'Mr. Ventilator,
    I am thankful to say that I am both able and willing to pay my creditors 20 shillings in the pound, and shall feel obliged, Mr. Ventilator, if you will state in your next paper that the Joseph Marks committed to prison by the County Court last week is not your obedient servant.

Joseph Marks, Cutler, High Street, Ryde. August 30th.

There was no further correspondence on the matter but the following year Marks' name crops up again in the *Ryde Ventilator*, always with a weather eye (and ear) open for a wee bit of hot gossip. The following news item appeared on June 1st 1872, eight months after the stranding of the *Underley*.

'Mr. Marks, a cutler of High Street, purchased some gunpowder from the wreck of the *Underley*. It proved worthless for explosive purposes and being harmless was taken to his home. On 28th May the police seized his whole stock, that fit for use being about 50 lbs. Mr. Marks has to appear before the magistrates on Monday. He is a member of the Ratepayers Association.

In the next edition there was a lengthy report of the case before the borough magistrates, of which a few extracts will have to suffice. *The Ventilator* had a reputation for its tirades against local officialdom.

A GUNPOWDER PLOT

'An Englishman in the present day has the satisfaction of knowing that he is surrounded on all sides with mantraps, and cannot be sure in any movement he makes that he is not rendering himself liable to penalties.

The ship *Underley* wrecked off Shanklin contained a large and miscellaneous cargo, amongst which was a quantity of gunpowder, and a portion thereof was sold to Mr. Marks, gunsmith of the High Street.

Our readers will form a pretty correct opinion of the material when we state that the lump about the size of an egg was thrown on a kitchen fire in the presence of the writer of these lines, and was not consumed for about a minute.'

72

Name board of the *Underley* sunk off Luccombe in September 1871 and (below) detail of the carving. The *Underley*'s name-board is now in the possession of Mr & Mrs K. Strevens of Carrigdene Farm, Bonchurch. (author's photographs)

We know of course that the gunpowder had been ruined by water during the wreck but it still seems a pretty foolhardy experiment for the reporter to have made! Apparently Joseph Marks carted the whole lot home, all two hundred pounds of it, storing it with over sixty pounds of top quality powder. Did this pillar of the local business community and member of the Ratepayers Association hope to unload the non-exploding explosive on unsuspecting customers? Or was there some legitimate use for it? We are not told, but the report does make the point that a dealer was allowed to store up to 200 lb of gunpowder on his premises. Marks now had 267 lb in his possession, just over the limit, and somebody tipped off the long arm of the law.

'On Tuesday the 28th of May one of our Borough Police Sergeants, armed with a search warrant, entered Mr Marks' premises and carried off this lot of rubbish . . . thus stopping for a time our townsman's business in that line . . .' [Perhaps the *Ventilator* should have put that a little differently] 'Mr. Marks was fined and put to the expense of obtaining legal aid. By whom this prosecution was instituted we know not – but the fact of an old soldier being selected to test the explosive power of the powder and no scientific person being called in to witness the experiment, gives a suspicious appearance thereto. Much larger quantities may be found stowed away in other establishments of the town than was seized by the police last week.'

If that last remark was correct it would seem that Ryde was in grave danger of being blown off the face of the Wight. The report ends 'If this prosecution was not malicious it was senseless in the extreme, and much better employment might be found for the police.'

Once again a shipwreck had gone on affecting lives on the island long after the storm which caused it had died away.

The *Hephzibah* was a small schooner laden with casks of codliver oil which had sailed in winter across the Atlantic Ocean from New-foundland to the English Channel. Her voyage was almost over when on November 17th 1871, she went ashore at Hanover Point. Local reports of her loss are short and uninformative. They do not tell us the state of wind or tide, the name of her skipper or to which port she was going, but we do know that the schooner did not require the services of the lifeboat, so we must assume that although hard on the beach she was at first in no danger of breaking up. Like the *Underley* a tug was

74

procured to pull her off the beach, and again like the *Underley* the attempt failed.

Saving the cargo of codliver oil then became extremely urgent and it seems that almost all was removed. The little report ends with the observation that the *Hephzibah* now laying on her side amongst the rocks would not long remain in one piece. Stuck on the beach she might be, but the little schooner was not alone. Three days after she was stranded, and only five hundreds away, the *Cassandra* joined her on the shore.

On Tuesday, November 21st 1871 the Isle of Wight branch of the RNLI held a sub-committee meeting at Brook lifeboat station. The coxswain, crew and helpers were paid their expenses for a practice call out during the previous quarter. Also paid was an outstanding bill for repainting the boat and her carriage. The last item debated that evening was the amount the sub-committee would recommend to be awarded to the boat crew and helpers at the wreck of the *Cassandra*. Considered for payment were thirty two men and six horses, (or rather the owners who had lent them for launching).

Cassandra was an iron barque of 710 tons, registered at Liverpool, owned by a Mr W Stewart Jones and under the command of Captain John Peters. She had a crew of twenty and, on this her last voyage, one passenger. The barque was on passage from Madras to London with a general cargo.

The *Cassandra* came ashore in Compton Bay, near Hanover Point, at half past two on the morning of Monday, November 20th 1871. Although the tide was on the ebb the squally wind and a heavy ground swell were both set into the shore. First of the rescue services to arrive on the scene were the Coastguards with their rocket line-throwing apparatus, with which they at once attempted to get a line aboard. Unfortunately the distance and high adverse wind proved to be beyond the capabilities of the rocket. The newly painted lifeboat was summoned from Brook and trundled along the Military Road by six horses. The road was not the tarmac highway it is today, but a trackway designed to enable foot soldiers and horsed officers to rapidly deploy along the coast.

Reaching Compton the boat was let down a recently constructed slipway and launched from the carriage into the sea. This could only be achieved by backing the horses into the water until the boat floated freely off the carriage. It was also the method used to recover the boat to bring it ashore and obviously needed a great deal of trust between man and animal and skilful handling to be successful.

When the boat at last reached the dangerously rolling wreck she was repeatedly slammed against the barque by the fierce ground swell. Onlookers and boat's crew alike expressed fears for the safety of the lifeboat and it did not escape without some damage. However, by six-thirty that morning about half of the *Cassandra*'s crew had been got into the lifeboat and taken ashore and barely an hour later the lifeboat was back again to the wreck to take off the captain and the rest of the crew.

In the meantime a good fire was stoked up in the resuscitating room adjoining the boat house at Brook, and the rescued, most of whom had managed to save a few clothes and other belongings, were dried out, warmed up, and given shelter from the inclement November weather. The solitary passenger, a sailor invalided home because of broken limbs, (he must have had a rough time), was lodged for a while at Brook Rectory until the local agent of the Shipwrecked Mariners Society, Mr Long of Yarmouth, had him conveyed by coach to Cowes to continue his journey to London.

By midday the lifeboat was back in her boathouse and prepared for the next call out, her new paint much the worse for wear. The weary crew and helpers dispersed to their homes to rest, not knowing how soon the news would come of another ship ashore.

Irex **1890**

The wreck of the *Irex* deserves a place in the records as a notable example of a rocket rescue. It also stirred up a great deal of controversy in the Isle of Wight.

When she was driven bow first on to the shore, with rocks all around and white towering cliffs looming over the ship, most of the men must have given themselves up for lost. Yet the rescuers did not leave the clifftop and the rescued did not have to enter the wild bone-smashing sea that was running.

The *Irex* was a new vessel, ship rigged and steel hulled, 2,248 registered tons, from Greenock and owned by a Captain Klink. Her first voyage, under the command of Captain Hutton, was planned to take the ship from Glasgow to Rio de Janeiro with a cargo of iron pipes. Each of the pipes, which were to be used in a new gas works at Rio, weighed nearly one and three quarter tons and the whole cargo totalled an estimated 3,600 tons.

She sailed from Glasgow on December 10th 1889, but running into heavy weather on the first day out the cargo shifted and had to return to Glasgow to be restowed. It was Christmas Eve before the *Irex* could sail again and the weather proved no better second time out. Christmas Day was spent sheltering in Belfast Lough and there she remained until New Year's Day 1890, when she began a painfully slow progress southwards. As one man later put it: We were beating about in the Irish Channel and two men were disabled, one with a broken leg and a broken arm and the other man with just a broken leg.

The stormy weather did not abate but the *Irex* pushed as far as the Bay of Biscay until further progress being impossible, Captain Hutton was obliged to run before the wind into the English Channel. When passing Falmouth the crew begged the mate to run the ship into port and land the injured men. The mate refused, saying he would sink the ship before considering such action and when the matter was referred to the captain he would consent only to transfer the injured men to any inward bound ship, though how he was to accomplish that in such awful seas he did not say.

So the *Irex* sailed on. One survivor recounted how, when the crew asked Captain Hutton where they were and where they were going, he would not answer. They were not to be ignorant for long. The Isle of

Wight barred the way ahead. The sailor added 'I reported land to the Captain and after my telling him we would not weather that light, [the Needles], he said, 'if we don't weather it we must go somewhere else'. But there was nowhere else for the *Irex* to go. The doomed ship entered Scratchells Bay and headed straight for the rocky shore, striking just after ten o'clock on Saturday night, January 25th 1890, having been at sea for a month.

The sea soon claimed its first victims. A crewman told his rescuers how he saw the captain alongside a boat giving orders for it to be prepared for launching when a huge sea swept over the poop and raced along the deck, taking with it Captain Hutton, the mate and the boatswain who were grouped together. They were not seen again. The story teller escaped the same fate by climbing into the rigging of the foremast where he remained until rescued. Throughout the night the crew held on grimly to whatever seemed immovable and it was not until daybreak that signals could be made to, and seen by, the light-house. All that time the seas had been pounding the *Irex* and taking a steady toll of the crew. In the deckhouse was the man with the broken leg, Harry by name, unable to climb into the rigging. It was thought the deckhouse would be a safe haven for old Harry, but the sea washed the unfortunate man right out of it, and he was eventually found dead, jammed among the pipes in the hold, the hatch covers having been smashed in by the sheer weight of water.

Another story brought off the wreck by survivors was that of a boy who refused to go aloft into the rigging. No inducements or entreaties by his mates would make him. He crouched on the deck protected by a hatchcoaming until it was demolished, then retreated along the deck to the next. He was drowned trying to find a safe refuge in the lee of the main hatchway. According to most of those rescued he was considered a 'very stupid boy'.

News of the disaster reached Totland Bay Lifeboat Station about ten o'clock on the Sunday morning and the boat was quickly launched. Also contacted was the rocket rescue team from Freshwater Fort, consisting of members of the local Coastguard. It proved impossible to row the lifeboat into the storm all the way from Totland and out through the Needles channel at any kind of useful rate, but the steam collier *Hampshire*, owned by a Mr Hill of Southampton, was lying off Totland pier sheltering from the storm and her master volunteered to tow the lifeboat through the Needles and into Scratchells Bay. When the line was slipped the lifeboat seemed about to make an immediate and successful rescue, but the attempt failed and twenty minutes later the *Hampshire* was signalled to take up the tow again which she did; the pair then returned to Totland.

In the following days a verbal storm broke out over the behaviour of the lifeboat's crew. The word cowardice was used, though most writers forgetting that the lifeboat had gone to within a few feet of the *Irex* in appalling conditions before having to turn away and those who wrote about True British Grit were not among those pulling oars. A century later we can only record that the lifeboat, played no part in the eventual rescue.

The rocket apparatus arrived on the cliff top around one o'clock on Sunday afternoon under the command of Mr Spilman, the chief officer. No time was lost preparing the gear and the first rocket was fired from the cliff ten minutes later. An eye witness said: 'It was a splendid shot by Coastguard Hallet. The rocket carried the line over the foremost rigging, which was then taken to the foretop where it was made fast' The main hawser was secured to the landward end of the light rocket line and willing hands hauled it aboard the *Irex* where it was firmly belayed to the foretop. From foremast to clifftop was about 400 feet and the prospect of being dragged along the distance in a breeches buoy, must have been daunting to all those left on *Irex*, but it was their only chance of being saved. The time was about 3.15 pm. and it was getting dark.

A seaman later said 'I was the man who went and got the rocket line. It was a grand shot and our hearts went up thirty degrees. After the work was finished I was sent ashore first to try the rope, because we wanted the injured men to come easy in their minds'. He was John Niccolls and he left the ship at 3.56 p.m.

His arrival at the clifftop was greeted by an outburst of cheering and applause from a large crowd of spectators braving the wild weather. Niccolls was hurried off to the Needles Fort where arrangements had been made to receive survivors. Under the direction of Master Gunner Lloyd, extra provisions had been brought in and fires lit in every room. A Doctor Dean who had volunteered his services was in attendance.

The next man taken there was 'a poor fellow who was fearfully injured, most of his limbs being broken,' but it was feared 'the poor fellow cannot recover'.

Irex aground in Scratchell's Bay, January 1890 (Carisbrooke
Castle Museum)

The only safe place on the *Irex* was in the rigging, well above the seas that still swept the ship from end to end. Those on board had to take advantage of every lull in the weather, however slight, to shift from mast to mast to attain the foremast from which the rescue gear was working. By five o'clock that evening seven men had been saved. Colonel Owen of the Royal Artillery, stationed at Golden Hill Fort, ordered his men to assist the Coastguard who had been without respite throughout the day on the exposed clifftop. The soldiers arrived at eight o'clock that evening being relieved at 10.30 p.m. by a fresh detachment.

The number of rescued men slowly mounted until just after midnight the twenty third man was brought across the perilous link between ship and shore. He, we are told, was a stowaway, there being apparently two on board in addition to the thirty four crew members. He told his rescuers that there were six men in a group forward and a lad aft, still on the ship. The six seamen forward were brought ashore during the early hours of Monday morning, but the lad was not so lucky as he did not get away till next day. He had been wrapped in a rug and lashed to the mainmast to save him from being washed away. His rescue was due to the bravery of one of his own shipmates, an unnamed coloured man, who having been saved himself went back aboard to help the boy, with Coastguard Machin who volunteered to go with him.

In the utter blackness of that winter's night the very air around the exhausted men on the clifftop seemed solid with flying spray, blinding them whenever they turned to face the cruel wind. The ship could not be seen but so long as that slender strumming lifeline remained the rescuers on the cliff knew *Irex* was still there in one piece, below them in the wild surf. Had she been a wooden ship she must have gone to pieces within a few hours, but luckily she was a Clyde built steel ship.

Of the possibly thirty six souls on the *Irex* when she struck, six were lost, but the others were saved in a rocket rescue without parallel. So great was nationwide interest in the wreck and the rescue that the Coastguards and soldiers were received by Queen Victoria at Osborne House. The injured who were too ill to be moved remained at the Needles Fort and here they were visited by the Princess Beatrice, the queen's daughter and a future Governor of the Isle of Wight. Richard Stern, the badly injured seaman, died about a week after his rescue and was buried at All Saints Church, Freshwater.

The dead captain of the *Irex* was widely condemned especially when it was disclosed that the log book for the ship could not be found, so no account remained of how Hutton had navigated the ship. One survivor sardonically commented: 'He must have been very wrong for us to be wrecked on the Isle of Wight on a voyage from Glasgow to Rio'.

View of the deck of the *Irex* after the storm (Carisbrooke Castle Museum)

George Henry and *Constance Ellen* 1894

It will be obvious to the reader by now that the greater number of shipwrecks around the Isle of Wight have occurred on the south-east and south-west coasts. Relatively few are recorded on the northern shores within the more sheltered Solent area. Though this stretch of water has had historic wrecks like *Mary Rose* and the *Royal George* these have generally been from other causes than stress of weather. Nevertheless entering the Solent has its hazards.

A ship's master sailing in through the Needles channel would have a wary eye on the rocks and massive headland to starboard and after 1753 he would know all about the Goose rock, concealed under the water between his vessel and the cliffs. In January 1753 the Captain of HMS *Assurance* did not know of it and lost his ship. Ahead would be the Hurst Narrows with fierce tide rips and to port the Shingles, a large, shifting shingle bank, which can be even today, a snare for the unwary.

Late in the afternoon on Wednesday, February 14th 1894 the schooner *George Henry* (in some records *George Henri*) grounded on the Shingles Bank opposite Totland Bay while bound for London to Dublin, under the command of Thomas Cooper, with a cargo of malt. The *George Henry* had been watched by the Coastguard for some time and, as soon as it became apparent she was in difficulties, they set out at six o'clock to render assistance, but none was required, although they stood by for more than four hours before returning to the Totland station around eleven o'clock that night. However before they had time to rest signal flares were observed coming from the Needles end of the Shingles Bank. A brigantine was in serious trouble.

The *Constance Ellen*, had also sailed from London to Ireland, and had already been six weeks on the passage with her cargo of iron and cement. Since leaving London the unfortunate vessel had been subjected to almost incessant storms and on Monday, February 12th, having reached St Aldhelm's Head, a few miles west of the island Captain Payne headed for the Needles, entered the Solent and sailed up to Lymington for shelter and provisions. There the *Constance Ellen* stayed until the afternoon of Wednesday February 14th leaving about two o'clock in a light westerly breeze which gradually freshened.

Disastrously, while beating her way out through the Needles, the wind suddenly died away, leaving her helpless in a strong tideway. Payne immediately dropped anchor but it would not hold and the fierce tide swept the ship onto the Bass Rock.

The Bass Rock is not known today, at least by that name. It does not appear on Admiralty charts, nor is it mentioned in pilot books, but it is named several times in reports of the stranding of the *Constance Ellen* so we must use it.

The brigantine grounded at about six o'clock and her crew immediately streamed a sea anchor at the end of sixty fathoms of rope to steady the ship and prevent her swinging broadside on to the racing tide. That night wind and sea began to work up and the brigantine's position became very uncomfortable and extremely critical. Flares were lit and answered by the coastguards. Mr. Watson the chief boatman, took the same crew to *Constance Ellen* that he did to *George Henry*, starting out about half past one on Thursday morning, January 15th. The coastguards remained by the brigantine until five o'clock and in conditions of very difficult communications Watson and Captain Payne agreed that, despite the high winds and rough seas, it might just be possible for a steam tug to pull the *Constance Ellen* clear. Her hull was, as yet, undamaged.

Victorian technology, in the form of the electric land line telegraph, could by this date be used to aid the shipwrecked mariner and if necessary outside of the normal Post Office hours. So at six o'clock when the coastguard boat returned to Totland a message was sent probably to Cowes, or perhaps Portsmouth, and by nine o'clock that morning the steam tug, *Hercules*, had arrived and was at work. The person sending the message would have had to go to either to Freshwater or Yarmouth as Totland had no telegraph office.

Meanwhile the RNLI Station at Totland, established in 1885 (it was moved in 1924 to its present location at Yarmouth) was alerted. There was a certain amount of rivalry between the Lifeboat men and the Coastguard where boat work was involved, but in general the coastguard boats were not intended to operate in gale conditions as the lifeboats were designed to do. So as conditions worsened the lifeboat men decided that the crews of the two stranded ships should be taken off. But even as they prepared to set out the *George Henry* broke free from the shingle holding her and floated away; out of our story. Her loss was not reported so we must assume that she found a safe haven to ride out the storm before continuing the voyage to Dublin. At midday on Thursday the lifeboat crew rowed into the teeth of the gale down the length of the Shingles almost to the Needles where they then swung round to drop downwind to the Bass Rock and the brigantine.

They stood by the *Constance Ellen* while the *Hercules* made two unsuccessful attempts to tow her off the rocks. It took slogging hard work and courage to rig the tows between the two ships and one can imagine the bitter disappointment as, at each attempt, the heavy hawsers parted, especially as the captain of the *Hercules* was on the traditional 'no cure, no pay' salvage contract and would be paid thirty pounds cash only if successful.

Heavy seas were now breakidng over the brigantine and great difficulty was experienced in getting Captain Payne and his crew of six seamen into the lifeboat. Nevertheless, they did take with them a few clothes and personal valuables. It is difficult to appreciate the trial of strength involved in rowing a pulling lifeboat against the elements in a howling storm. Yet men did it and, then as now, there was no shortage of volunteers.

Further attempts to refloat the *Constance Ellen* were made a day or so later and happily were successful. From then on she led, so far as we know, an uneventful life until one day in November 1901, in an easterly gale, she failed to get between the piers at South Shields on the Tyne. With most of her sails carried away and almost out of control Captain Robinson, who then commanded her, ran her on to the beach. The local Volunteer Life Brigade with their rocket apparatise were soon on the scene and for the second time all her crew were saved.

They lived to sail again but this time the ship was a total loss.

Alcester 1897

In researching almost any shipwreck it is a difficult task to reconcile the different reports and accounts which often contain widely differing and contradictory statements. Judging just what were the true facts is not easy and sometimes impossible. In the end the result is presented to the reader as accurately as the source material allows, but even at best comes as a second or even third hand account of events few of us, thankfully, are ever likely to experience.

However, nothing is second hand in the following account of the loss of the *Alcester* and its veracity can be relied upon, because every word was written by her master, A. D. Haws.

The *Alcester* was owned by his mother and Captain Haw's letter to her was written eleven days after the ship was wrecked on the Atherfield Ledge. As well as providing a reliable source of facts this letter is a good piece of descriptive writing and it also gives us a good insight into the captain, a quiet reflectful man of great personal courage who inspired considerable loyalty in his men. *Alcester*'s mate stayed on the ship because her master stayed.

The earlier departure of his crew was but common sense. The *Alcester* had been aground for almost a day. She was badly damaged and full of water and it was obvious she would never move again. The lifeboat was standing by and there was time for the captain too to pack a few treasured possessions, including his father's sextant, the loss of which was later much lamented. But so long as her master remained on board the ship was not abandoned to any salvor out for rich pickings.

However, if at the end, the *Alcester* and her cargo could not be saved, Haws' primary concern continued to be the financial well-being of her owners. Wages for the crew ceased the moment they left the ship according to the immemorial custom of the sea. (There was a great public outcry when it became common knowledge that all pay for the seamen of the Titanic stopped the instant she sank at 2.20 am April 15th 1912). We can allow ourselves a wry smile at the thought of Captian Haws and the mate, sitting quietly at the table in the after saloon, working out the crew's wages while around them the ship was slowly, but very noisily, breaking up.

Surely they were both fine men, hard when occasion demanded but never asking of any man what they could not do themselves. The letter lifts just a corner of the veil that divides us and our uncertain world from Captain Haws, who had no doubts about his.

Fern Grove
March 2nd 1897

Dear Mother.

I am taking a sheet of foolscap to write to you, as I have no ruled letter papers and I have a long letter to write about the loss of the ship.

We went on shore on Friday night, 19th of Feb at 5 pm in a dense fog, on the Atherfield Ledge, Isle of Wight. It is on the west side of the Island. There were a couple of steamers in there also, but they saved themselves, having steam power, but we were stuck. We bumped all Friday night and Saturday morning. A tug came and in trying to get her off he finished her, as the hawser parted and a large rock got amidships under and made a hole in her that soon filled her.

The crew came aft and wanted to leave her, so I signalled for the lifeboat, I remainded by her and the mate would not leave me. So we remained. Lloyds agent tried to coax me out of her, but I would not go, and he told me there would be a heavy ground swell but no wind, that the fishermen had told him so. I examined the glasses and found all right. So, we decided to remain.

The mate and I got some tea for ourselves. The Jute was swelling with the wet and bursting the beams and forcing the decks up, we would hear them continually going like the report of a gun. It used to make the mate and I smile when Lloyds agent would jump as a beam broke under his feet.

After tea, the mate and I sat down to make out the sailors account of wages. We sat there figuring for a while, with an occasional beam cracking under our feet and the sea sweeping by with a roar until at last I said to the mate, 'Let us get on deck and see what is going on'. So the mate went up on the poop and sung out to me to come up; that it was frightful up there.

I went up, and the sea all around was like a snow field. So I said we must get onto the forecastle as she was taking the sea on the quarter. From there we were driven into the forerigging by the rising sea, and we remained half way up the rigging until the sea sweeping over her was reaching up to us. So then we got into the foretop, and burnt blue lights for the lifeboat, not expecting that it could be launched in such a sea. But they answered us and attempted to launch the boat, but, as we anticipated, found it impossible.

We loosed the top gallant staysail and I ripped it across with my knife, and we hauled it round the topmast rigging for a weather cloth.

The seas were coming over aft and sweeping right forward and over the bows, smashing and destroying all in their way. About half an hour after we

87

were driven out of the cabin, a sea came over and washed away the lifeboats aft, and shirls [?] and bridge in one smash. The mate asked me what it was, I told him I thought it was the boats as I saw something white coming along which I thought was the remains of a lifeboat.

We had one lifeboat hanging in the davits ready for lowering, the mate wanted to take that and take our chance of driving up on the beach, but I told him we could not live to reach it and if we did we would drown on the beach in the surf. It would look well in the morning to find us both drowned and the masts standing alright. That had occurred too often and as long as she held together I meant to stick to her. We both had cork lifebelts on, which we had got out of the forecastle.

I would not have minded the attempt in the daytime, because there would have been plenty of people on the beach to haul us out as we were hurled up by the sea. But at night we would have drowned to a certainty.

About eleven it was blowing very hard and everything seemed to be breaking up. We both thought we were done for so I said to the mate 'I hope you will forgive me for causing you to lose your life by remaining by the ship'. That is the time to try men, so he says, 'Don't let that lay on your mind sir. I have no one to look to me, you have a wife and children. Don't trouble about me, I am all right' That was said when neither of us expected to see daylight as the gale was increasing.

Many men would have said, well if you had not stuck by the ship I would not have been here, it is your fault. So he said, 'I am going to sleep to forget my misery'. He said 'I am played out'.

So I got him curled up in by the mast with the stay sail around him and told him I would keep watch and see if the masts commenced to go, so as to make an attempt to reach the bowsprit end. As soon as they commenced to go we would have slid down the jib stays onto the bowsprit, as we could not have lived on the main deck or forecastle head to reach there.

As we were sitting there watching her, he said, 'Well sir, she has served us faithfully often and brought us safely through many a danger, and if she pulls us through this she will have served us to the bitter end'. And there is no mistake she was true to the last.

After midnight the tide turned, which made the water smoother, and I got more reckless to it. I found myself dozing off, so I roused myself and lit another cigar. I suppose I smoked about a dozen cigars that night as one must watch.

About 2 am the gale commenced to moderate and at 3.30 am we made further signals for the lifeboat to let them know we were still alive. As there was not so much water on deck, and the mate was parched with thirst we came down on deck to try to get in the cabin and see if there was any fresh water anywhere. Well, it was a sight, one mass of wreckage piled up

The *Alcester* broken in two on Atherfield Ledge, 1897 (Carisbrooke Castle Museum)

forward on the port side, deck bust up, hatches off and cargo out of the hold.

We made our way aft and clambered onto the poop as the door leading to cabin off the main deck was locked. The ladders were gone, but that did not stop us. We got onto the poop and found all cleaned out there; skylight smashed up, and pilot house washed away and ventilators and all clean sweep except the wheel.

I went down the companionway and when I reached the cabin I sung out that the place was full of water, and to be careful as I could feel everything washing against me. I got to the door leading to the passage out on deck on which his room was situated, but it opened inwards and found it had been forced through so it would go neither way. The mate said, 'Let me try it', so I struck a match and he tried to kick it through, but without success. I said, 'Come out of this, it makes me feel sick. This is no place for us'.

So we made our way on the poop and forward onto the forecastle, and after being there for a while we went back into the foretop again and remained there until daylight when we came down for good.

The mate and I had a rummage around and such a scene of desolation I never saw. I have seen a few ships that have been cleaned by hurricanes in the East Indies, but this beats all. I think if anyone had heard us they would have thought we had gone crazy as we could not help laughing at the way the inside of the forecastle was cleaned out; and the galley. We could not find anything, stove or anything else. All gone

We got a capstan bar and made our way aft and down into the cabin and soon battered down the door and got into the mate's room. We found only two feet of water there. We got a drink of water and then opened the main deck door. The mate then got an augur and we bored holes in the deck to see if we could drain any of it into the hold.

We saw the lifeboat coming off so the mate packed a few things. I went after my chronometers and ships papers. I found some, but not all. Such a mess in the cabin, bulkheads down, stove, settees, one of the steering compasses; stands and all, washed down through the companionway. We went into my room, all the drawers out and floating around, clothes around everywhere.

Then I examined the ship. I found the jute had swelled so much that the decks were all burst and forced up around the main hatch as high as the top of the bulwarks. The after end of the house raised so much that it sloped forward. I told the mate that she was properly done for, that her back was broke, and she would not last much longer.

So we got a few things along, and when the lifeboat came alongside as she ran on a sea, the coxswain sung out, 'Jump, jump for your lives'. Needless to say we did not wait to get our things but left chronometers, papers and all behind. We got ashore alright amidst much cheering from the people lining the cliffs. As the mate said, we were stared at like wild animals. No doubt we looked a sight with long gum boots on, old clothes and lifebelts.

A couple of hours after we left her, she broke in two amidships. John got down in the forenoon and as the sea got smooth we launched a boat and went off in the afternoon to her. The mate and I started hunting among the wreckage for our gear. I found the ship's papers and the mate's bag, and he found my overcoat and that was all. I had lost Father's sextant, which I set more store by than anything else. The watch is alright, as I had it on. The pen Cliss gave me I am now writing with as I had it in my waistcoat pocket. I had been writing with it when we had to quit so I had put it in my waistcoat pocket. So we had a time of it.

Lloyds agent came over Monday to me and got me by the hand and said, 'Captain, no one has the least idea what you and the mate went through Saturday night'. He said, 'I did not go off until Monday and when I climbed over the rail and saw the decks, I could not stand it, it fairly turned me sick and I got back into the boat and could not remain on board her'. He said, 'She looked bad Saturday afternoon when I wanted you to come ashore, but I had no conception of what it really was like after'.

Now and again during the night the mate would say, 'What is that?' as a report like a gun would be heard; only another beam gone, breaking up all the time.

The mate and I have lost all our clothes and instruments. I had no insurance on my things this time, so I have lost all.

There have been some photos taken which I will send to you when I get them. The inquiry will come off next week I expect. So do not be surprised if you do not get a letter until then.

I was surprised when John told me you had made over the shares of the ships to me, as I had quietly made up my mind to hear no more about it. I see by your letter that you misunderstood what I wrote. If you have the letter, read it again and see if it is not twenty years instead of two. What I meant was that by that time we would both probably be dead, and it would not matter to either. You will perceive that I came nearly to going in less than the two years you mention in your letter.

As long as you do not require it, Mother, I shall feel thankful to have it as it may give me a chance to see if I can remain on shore.

I shall close now, with much love from all

Your affectionate son,

A. D. Haws.

Captain Haws did not have to wait long for the inquiry which was held at Liverpool on March 10th and 11th. It found that he alone was to blame for the wreck of the ship and suspended his certificate for three months. It was a small blemish on a creditable career. Haws who was born at Levis in Canada in 1862 came to Britain at the age of 14 and had his first command at 21. He died in 1926 aged 64. The company, R. C. Haws and Co., were renowned for their fine ships. The *Alcides*, a near sister of *Alcester*, while under the command of Captain L. C. Dart sailed from Hong Kong to New York in the splendid time of eighty three days. Leaving Hong Kong on December 18th, 1894 she arrived in New York on March 11th 1895 after a midwinter passage across the Atlantic.

3

A Naval Catastrophe

The Loss of
HMS Eurydice 1878

Today's efficient and highly trained Royal Navy is the direct result of sweeping changes in social conditions that began to make themselves felt from about 1830. Harsh conditions on the lower deck for those who had to haul and heave were slowly ameliorated, so that while life was still hard, genuine concern for the ordinary seaman's welfare was expressed by an increasing number of senior officers.

Britain always had difficulty in finding enough seamen to crew her warships in times of hostility. One difficulty, apart from poor conditions, was that men recruited for a war were discharged as soon as it was over. The evil Press Gang system intended to overcome the reluctance to serve aboard Royal Navy ships, was never a satisfactory solution to the manning problem and it was not used after 1815. By this time it was realised that if the uncertainty could be removed from the terms of employment, perhaps men could be persuaded to look on service in the Navy as a career and with this new professional outlook a training and educational system had to be established. This commenced with *HMS Excellent* in 1830, the Navy's gunnery training ship until superseded in 1864 by a shore station of the same name on Whale Island in Portsmouth Harbour. *Excellent* was but the first of many training establishments among which was the ill-fated *HMS Eurydice*.

The *Eurydice* was a wooden fully rigged three masted sailing ship of 921 tons displacement, a 6th rate man o' war classed as a frigate. She was built in 1843, mounting 26 guns (twenty four 32 pdrs and two 12 pdrs) and was considered by many to be the smartest and fastest frigate in the service. In 1861, still in her original build state, she became a general training ship and remained so until 1876. During that year and early 1877, in John White's yard at Cowes, *Eurydice* was converted into a sail training ship for seamen, not as so often wrongly quoted, a training ship for boys only. Many were adult married men with families and they were aboard simply because they were seamen under instruction.

The Admiralty rightly considered the best place to learn the trade of seaman was in a ship at sea on a long voyage, and *HMS Eurydice* was returning from Bermuda after such a voyage when lost off the Isle of Wight. Her normal crew, as a frigate, would have been about 120 men, but as a floating classroom accommodation was found for nearly 300 men under training, together with another 30 or 40 fully experienced as basic crew and instructors.

HMS Eurydice commissioned at Portsmouth in February and after initial working up sailed for Bermuda on November 13th, 1877. By this date sail was rapidly retreating in the face of steam power and the Royal Navy had only a few 'pure' sailing ships in commission, nearly all of those engaged in harbour duties or training.

Nevertheless, the skills of handling square rigged sail were still considered essential to qualify a recruit as able seaman and to that end the programme of *HMS Eurydice* was organised. It unfortunately led to one of the Royal Navy's most harrowing peace-time disasters.

The afternoon of Sunday, 24th March, 1878 was bright and mild, the fine weather heralding the coming end of winter, and bringing out a number of people to enjoy a quiet stroll along the seafront of Ventnor. About four o'clock all eyes were turned to a pleasant sight when, close to the shore, *HMS Eurydice* was seen bowling along under full sail at a fine rate.

However, it was obvious that weather conditions were rapidly changing, the sky darkening and the wind rising. Old salts along the sea front remarked that the ship would soon have to shorten sail, but there was no sign of hands going aloft to reef. Suddenly the wind shrieked across the water and a heavy snow storm completely obscured the frigate and sent the watchers scuttling for shelter. They did not see *HMS Eurydice* again. She had capsized and sunk and of over 300 souls aboard her only two lived to tell of it.

Captain William Langworthy Jenkin, master of the schooner *Emma* bound from Newcastle to Poole with a cargo of coal, looked anxiously behind him and did not much like what he saw. *Emma* had Shanklin Head four or five miles to starboard and was carrying a good spread of canvas, too much, thought Jenkin, to be safe in the dirty weather racing up behind over his starboard quarter. Shouting to make himself heard above the rising wind Captain Jenkin ordered his crew to take in sail, leaving only the jib drawing. With the captain himself at the helm there were just five other men to carry out the order, but before they could finish the job the storm was upon them and the task had to be completed in the blinding snow. The storm lasted for about half an hour and when passed left conditions of good visibility with only a moderate wind. The sea which had been whipped up to white capped breakers rapidly moderated, but it remained bitterly cold.

Thankful that his ship had survived the sudden squall, William Jenkin looked around and could hardly believe his eyes. He observed wreckage which was moving down channel on a strongly ebbing tide, but what shocked him was to see the royals of a ship, still on the yards, flapping just above the water.

Jenkin sent a man into the rigging who reported that he could see a man in the water. *Emma* at once altered course towards him, and when close enough lowered a boat to pick him up and to search amongst the jumble of wreckage for other survivors, if any. *Emma*'s boat crew looked amongst the deck lockers and spare spars which littered the surface of the sea, the hundred and one things that once had an exact place on a well-run ship, but which were now floating in utter confusion on the choppy sea. They found only four more men in the water and hurried back to the *Emma* with them.

While some of his crew did all they could to revive the rescued seamen, Jenkin, with his schooner's colours at half mast, made for Ventnor. *Emma*'s distress signal was recognised and a boat carrying a doctor put off from the shore, followed by the Coastguard boat with Captain Roach, RN, Inspecting Commander of St. Catherine's Division, on board. By a freak chance Captain Roach knew one of the five men taken from the icy water, and he knew also the ship in which he was serving. Roach recognised Lieutenant Tabor of *HMS Eurydice*, but there was no warm greeting of friends, for Tabor was dead.

Roach immediately telegraphed Admiral Fanshawe, Commander-in-Chief at Portsmouth, who at once despatched a steamer to search for any other survivors who might be clinging to wreckage. Admiral Fanshawe also informed the Admiralty who at once communicated the news to the Queen who was then at Osborne. Queen Victoria responded with a telegram which read: 'The Queen is deeply grieved to hear of the loss of the *Eurydice*. Her Majesty anxiously asks for further details.' A second telegram to the First Lord of the Admiralty said: 'The Queen would ask Mr. Smith [W. Heckstall Smith of bookshop fame] to make known her grief at the terrible calamity to the *Eurydice*, and her heartfelt sympathy with the afflicted friends and relatives.' Copies were posted at the dockyard gates in Portsmouth and eagerly read by the crowds.

The only living survivors, men named Cuddiford and Fletcher, were taken to the Cottage Hospital at Bonchurch and placed under the care of Doctor James Williamson who declared that they were 'doing fairly well.'

HMS Eurydice had sailed from Portsmouth for the West Indies on November 13th 1877, under the command of Captain Marcus Hare who previously had commanded the training ships *HMS St. Vincent* at Portsmouth and *HMS Boscawen* at Portland. After exercising with other ships she left Bermuda on March 6th 1878 and nothing was heard of her until she was reported by the coastguard at Bonchurch at 3.30 pm on that fateful Sunday afternoon, sailing hard for her home port, 'under all plain sail and with her port stunsails set on the foretopmast and main topmast'. Her commander clearly intended to arrive in a smart fashion at Spithead anchorage before nightfall.

A heavy bank of cloud was coming down from the north west and the barometer was rapidly falling. Such wind as there was came from the west and blew onto the port quarter of the ship. The south east coast of the Isle of Wight, extending from Blackgang to Shanklin, has a high ridge of downland reaching to about 500 feet above the sea. This high land affords a deceptive shelter for ships close inshore. From the direction from which *HMS Eurydice* was sailing she would be in smooth water, sheltered by the downs, until rounding Dunnose Point. At about ten minutes before four o'clock the wind suddenly veered from west to north west and sweeping down with gale force from the high ground, and struck the *Eurydice* on her port bow.

The sole survivors of the *Eurydice* tragedy, Able Seaman Cuddiford and Ordinary Seaman Fletcher (Carisbrooke Castle Museum)

Exactly what happened at that crucial moment is not known because the swirling snow storm hid her from view, but it seems probable that she was flung on her beam ends, never recovered and sank within seconds taking most of the three hundred aboard down with her.

An inquest on the bodies recovered, those of Lieutenant Francis Hope Tabor, Captain Louis Ferrier, Royal Engineers, and Ordinary Seaman Daniel Bennett was held on Tuesday, March 26th. It was to have been at the Queens Hotel on Ventnor Esplanade, but the press coverage it attracted, together with the number of official representatives, made it necessary to move to the larger Royal Hotel.

After formal evidence of identification the first witness was one of the only two men now alive who could give first hand testimony of what happened aboard. He was Able Seaman Benjamin Cuddiford, one of the thirty experienced ratings who made up the regular ship's company. He told the coroner's jury how, about two o'clock on Sunday afternoon when the ship was off the Isle of Wight, they had set the lower stunsails, and then had all sails set except the topgallant stunsails. The weather was fine and bright and there was a moderate wind just abaft the beam. Then he described the moment the squall hit:-

'Between half past three and four o'clock they called the lower watch to take in the lower stunsail; the weather looking dirty to windward. The sail was taken in and then orders were given to take in the royals. The squall caught us before the royals were in and the Captain ordered the men down for their own safety; the royals were lowered but not furled. Then, the Captain gave orders to let go the maintopsail and mainsheet. This was done and the next order from the Captain was "If you can't let it go – cut it" but I don't know to what the order referred.'

The ship was then almost on her beam ends, and the water up to the men's waists. I was on the quarter deck netting, I got there to get on the weather side of the ship. I could see her keel and her sails were in the water. She righted again and I saw her mizzen top come out of the water. The ship was sinking forwards taking a body of men which had been on her bottom. Just as the water got abreast of the mainmast, she again went over until her keel was out of the water.

I stuck to the ship. The Captain had given orders to get the cutter clear, and we cleared one rope by cutting it, but the water encroached upon us. The Captain was about six or seven feet from me. I then jumped into the water and swam past the two doctors. They were drowning but I could not help them.

I swam to the round life buoy and went to the assistance of others with pieces of wood and spars. The Captain was on the vessel when I jumped and she must have gone down immediately. I saw six men clinging to an upturned boat and they asked if there was any hope. I said the best thing they could do was to keep their spirits up. I turned my back to the squall and the other man (Fletcher) was near me. I was in the water for almost an hour and twenty minutes, and although conscious I felt giddy and staggered when I tried to stand on the schooner's deck.

In answers to questions by the jury Cuddiford agreed that the gun deck ports were open, as was usual in such weather as that before the storm. The ports were about five feet above the water when the ship was on an even keel. The guns were well secured.

There was one watch below when the order was first given to reduce sail. On a sail training ship like the *Eurydice*, with its huge crew, there would have been about 150 men off watch. There was no order given for 'all hands' to shorten sail and it was not usual to give such an order on a naval ship where the watch on deck were quite sufficient, in normal circumstances, to carry out any order. We must assume that when Captain Hare realised conditions were anything but normal, it was too late.

The inquest questioned Cuddiford about the safety equipment carried by the *Eurydice*, and he said she had four quarter boats and a galley which, however, was damaged and unusable; the four boats were well secured and none were launched. Distributed about the upperdeck and quarterdeck were five life-buoys and twelve life-belts. The *Eurydice* also carried two cutters, one to port and one to starboard; the normal crews for them being eleven men in one and thirteen in the other and there should have been a life-belt for each of the cutter's crews as 'that was the regulations'. The cutters were stowed bottoms up and Cuddiford was unable to say if the life-belts were in place or not. A total of five life-buoys and twelve lifebelts ready for use, six usable boats, well lashed down, and twenty-four life-belts stowed in the inverted cutters does not seem a great amount of equipment on a training ship that regularly went to sea with over 300 men on board. The point however was not pursued and for many

99

HMS Eurydice in dry dock at White's Yard, Cowes in 1877
(Charles Taylor collection)

years afterwards the use of ships without adequate lifesaving appliances continued, until the disaster of the *Titanic* in 1912, in fact. Given the speed with which the *Eurydice* went down more lifebelts might not have been of much use, but would surely have saved one or two more lives.

The other survivor who gave evidence was Sidney Fletcher, just turned 19 years of age, who had served as Ordinary Seaman in the *Eurydice* for six months. He was below, getting his tea in order to be ready to go on watch at eight bells (four o'clock) when he heard a rush of water coming through the ports. Just before that the ship had given a lurch.

Fletcher ran up on deck and let go the main topsail halyards but by that time water was coming over the lee nettings. He clawed his way over to the weather side, as Cuddiford had done, and walked right aft on the side of the ship below the line of her ports. Reaching the quarter he could see the frigate's keel out of the water.

The wind was blowing hard and driving the snow before it in a blizzard; the seas were breaking over the ship, which was so far over that the yards were in the water. Fletcher last saw Captain Hare still on the quarter trying to organise men to clear away the cutter, but the ship was sinking fast and Ordinary Seaman Fletcher took his chance by jumping into the sea.

About thirty yards from the sinking ship he found a lifebelt which he said he thought had fallen from the cutter. Holding grimly to the lifebelt Fletcher turned his attention to what he could see of the stricken vessel, now almost under water. He saw Sub Lieutenant Edmunds take off his coat and jump overboard, but the unfortunate young officer disappeared at once. Also standing on the ship was Mr Tabor, and even at a time like that Fletcher noticed that the lieutenant was not wearing his hat. He afterwards saw Tabor clinging to a deck locker and also Brewer, the boatswain, who floated past supported by a life belt. He asked Brewer in which direction he thought land was but he received no answer. As the snow cleared he saw the island about half a mile away and the schooner *Emma* standing towards the wreckage.

In answer to a question by the Coroner, Sidney Fletcher said that apart from himself and one or two others none of the 160 or so men below deck at the time could have reached the upper deck. He only did so because he was at the foot of the hatchway. He could hear the trapped men crying out and screaming. Among them was one man in irons, a prisoner in the ship's cells.

The inquest then turned to the question of the stability of the ship itself which became a principal factor of investigation. But although questions were asked they were never satisfactorily answered.

Coroner Had you a sufficient quantity of ballast on board?
Fletcher A great quantity of our ballast was water.
Coroner Which was being consumed during the voyage?

Fletcher Yes.

Coroner Do you know if there was a large quantity of water in her on Sunday afternoon before this happened?

Fletcher No, I cannot tell.

Foreman You had not been put on a short allowance of water?

Fletcher No sir.

Coroner Were the guns or stores displaced previously?

Fletcher No, not that I know of.

Mr Harvey Do you really know whether the water formed part of the ballast?

Fletcher I know we had water on board and I always understood that it was partly carried as ballast. I do not know that we had any concrete and iron on board as ballast.

The court then recalled Benjamin Cuddiford who was examined by Mr Henry Owen, the Admiralty Agent as to what ballast the *Eurydice* had.

Cuddiford She had her proper ballast for the tonnage of the vessel.

Owen What is this about the water being reckoned as ballast?

Cuddiford She had two tiers of tanks and the lower tier was never touched or disturbed in any way.

Cuddiford no doubt believed his answer to be absolutely true and it was accepted at the inquest, but true it was not as subsequent inquiries showed. We have to remember, although Cuddiford was an intelligent man who had been in the *Eurydice* since her commissioning thirteen months previously he occupied only a lowly status. If Captain Hare believed the water ballast tanks to have been disposed in the ship as Cuddiford had thought them to be, he too was greatly mistaken. But was he fatally and culpably mistaken? That question was never very deeply examined, but the questioning of the able seaman continued.

Owen Had she sufficient ballast in her without the water?

Cuddiford She had sufficient ballast in her without reckoning the water or her stores but when the water and the stores became light the vessel sailed lighter and became more lively, and when she gave lurches, as she often did, she would knock us off our feet to leeward.

Owen She had the reputation of being a lively vessel had she not?

Cuddiford No, I did not know that she had.

Owen The lower tier of tanks being full of water and never touched would add to her ballast as a matter of course?

Cuddiford Yes, of course it would.

Owen At any time during the period you have been on board the *Eurydice* have you ever heard anything said about her ballast having been shifted or interfered with in any way?

Cuddiford No. had it been shifted I must have known.

The Coroner then turned to the weather, asking Cuddiford if he had heard of any sudden fall having taken place in the barometer. The witness said he had not. No. Had there been any fall when the barometer was read at eight o'clock on Sunday morning he would have known of it as he was close by Doctor Murdock when he took the reading. No one thought to ask if there had been any barometer readings in the subsequent eight hours before the disaster.

The inquest turned to William Langworthy Jenkin, Master of the schooner *Emma*, of Padstow, proceeding at the time from Newcastle to Poole. Although Jenkin himself did not see the *Eurydice* before the storm a member of his crew, George Parkinson, did and said that as far as he could see the training ship was carrying all her sails, but he did not think she had too much on when he first saw her. He estimated the training ship was only a mile offshore whereas *Emma* was at least four miles out.

The Coroner asked Jenkin if he had any warning of the storm. Although he replied laconically that it looked rather bad to windward before it came on, it was obviously sufficient warning to make him take precautions.

Coroner Did you make an alteration to your sails in consequence?

Jenkin Yes, we hauled down the flying jib, the main topmast stay sail and the gaff topsail. We lowered away at the mainsail, the fore topgallant sail and checked the various halyards, we afterwards lowered the foresail.

Coroner What sail had you then set?

Jenkin We had only the standing jib set properly.

Coroner Did you consider the squall was sufficiently violent to capsize the *Eurydice*, she being under full sail?

Jenkin No, I should think not. I was surprised when I found the *Eurydice* had gone down. I thought I was picking up a boat's crew.

The *Emma* was a topsail schooner of only 137 tons, very much smaller than the *Eurydice*, whose small crew of but six men, including the captain, could not get all the sails off before the squall struck her. The crew had to work in the snow storm to reduce to the single headsail that Jenkin thought sufficient – or safe. Captain Jenkin then related how they had lifted five men from the water. One, Bennett, was dead and two more expired before he could get them ashore, Only Cuddiford and Fletcher surviving.

Doctor James Mann Williamson told how he went on board the schooner and, assisted by a Doctor Morton, used every means to restore the two dying men but without success. Captain Jenkin had previously said that he had no stimulants, meaning brandy or other spirits, on board to administer to anybody rescued from the water, a fact which provoked a great deal of criticism. Doctor Bruce Williamson, of Ventnor, son of the medical witness recalled (in about 1975) that his father had often told him that he could have revived the others with spirits. At the time an angry correspondent in *The Globe* wrote: It appears that the master of the *Emma* when he got the men on board could not apply the usual restoratives because his was what is known as a 'temperance craft'. That is to say the *Emma* did not carry any stimulants for her crew, and what is more serious, the medicine chest contained neither brandy or any kind of spirits. From the facts it appears urgently necessary for the Board of Trade to take immediate steps to prevent such omissions in future. The idiosyncracies of the master of a vessel should not be allowed to imperil the lives of his crew or anyone. Under the circumstances, everyone, whether a total abstainer or not, must lament this sad example of too much temperence.

It may well have been true, but spirits would not have saved the rest of the three hundred sailors and it is certain that there were more pressing questions to be asked about the loss of HMS *Eurydice*. Unfortunately they never were adequately pursued.

The Coroner in his summing up said the evidence showed there was not too much sail being carried and Captain Hare had acted in good time. As to whether the capsizing might have been due to want of sufficient ballast, Cuddiford had proved that the ship had the proper amount. With equally uncritical obedience, the jury returned a verdict that the three dead men were drowned due to the sinking of the *Eurydice* and that no blame could be attached to the captain, officers and men of the ship. Modern public opinion, used to the glaring spotlight of investigative journalism, would certainly not have been satisfied with such an unquestioning conclusion. Unfortunately its subsequent court martial did little better and questions in the House of Commons produced equally unsatisfactory answers.

Why did HMS *Eurydice* capsize in that squall of short duration while other ships in the area did not?

As we have seen the stability of the ship was called into question at the inquest. Ordinary Seaman Fletcher, from what he had heard, was under the impression that the ballast of the ship was principally the water held in tanks below the usual stores of the ship, but Able Seaman Cuddiford said the ship had her proper ballast and that the lower tier of tanks was never disturbed, a version fully accepted by the Coroner.

Some considerable consternation was caused when it was made public that the lower tier of water tanks had never been fitted!

This disturbing fact was brought to light when the dockyard super-intendent examined the drawings of the *Eurydice* in preparation for raising the vessel. It comes as no surprise to find that a whitewash campaign immediately commenced. Experts were quoted as saying there would be no loss of stability, the only result would be to make her more 'lively' and that, in a voyage as long as the *Eurydice* had just completed, the draught would be lessened only by about ten inches.

Fuel was added to the fire when it was disclosed that the gun ports were only about five feet above the waterline, and that a comparatively small heel of eighteen degrees would take the ports under water. The ship could be expected to heel further than that with only a moder-ately strong wind abeam. Small wonder she laid her yards in the sea when struck by the storm while carrying full sail.

In reply to questions in the House of Commons the First Lord of the Admiralty stated that the amount of ballast in the *Eurydice* was thirty tons, the amount she had always carried and there was no reason to suppose any was removed. It is obvious that here he was referring only to the fixed ballast of iron pigs or concrete, the existence of which Fletcher was unaware. When pressed, the First Lord of the Admiralty added a few more details to his statement. In place of her original 26 guns, HMS *Eurydice*, as a sail training ship, was equipped with only two 64 pounders, but her water ballast was increased from 102 tons to 117 tons. Smith also said that the vessel's draught was 16 feet 6 inches but one must assume this figure to be correct only at her fully laden condition. It would obviously be much less at the end of a lengthy voyage.

HMS *Eurydice* and a similar ship, *HMS Modeste*, were built to the designs of an Admiral Elliot and those ships differed in one important aspect from other ships of similar size in the Royal Navy. It was noted these appeared to stand higher above the water than other vessels of their class and they drew considerably less water. At 16 ft 6 ins the draught of *HMS Eurydice* was less by about four feet than that normal for ships of 900 to 1,000 tons. A correspondent in the *Isle of Wight Observer* for April 6th 1878 wrote:

I once owned a fast merchant ship of 341 tons [just over a third of the size of the *Eurydice*] and in best sailing trim she drew over 16 feet of water, and today our cutter yacht of 111 tons draws 14 feet. This small amount of draught of water coupled with greater height out of the water and the fact that both the ballasting power of the provisions and water for 300 men in a voyage across the Atlantic must have been materially reduced, are, I think, reasons why this fine ship should not recover herself when struck by so exceptionally a sudden and so unusually heavy a squall.

It begins to look suspiciously as if the eventual loss of the *Eurydice* was built into the ship during her conversion at John White's yard in Cowes and it was not a question of if she would capsize, but when! And in the course of handling her through a thirteen month commission had her commander not become aware of any cranky tendencies?

By the end of March plans were well advanced for the salvage of the *Eurydice*. Two hundred coffins were prepared at Haslar Naval Hospital at Gosport and a large plot of ground marked off in the cemetery.

On Saturday April 6th the steam paddle tug *Camel*, 484 tons, cruised around the wreck in a last look for bodies released by the tides and none being found the go-ahead was given to start operations. A lighter, the *Dromedary*, was moored over the wreck but owing to gale force winds she had to slip her anchors and move out to sea, returning when the strong winds abated. Monday, April 8th should have seen the first lifting craft, *Pearl*, brought into position, but high wind again prevented any progress. A letter to *The Times* expressed public dissatisfaction at the rate of progress but many more weeks were due to go by before the job was finished. Articles of clothing now began to appear on the beaches of the Isle of Wight and the sad, sodden name

HMS Eurydice alongside at White's Yard, Cowes where she was converted to a training ship. The alterations may have contributed to her fatal loss (Charles Taylor collection)

tags reveal their late owners – Ordinary Seamen William French, John Kelly and H. Scull.

The approach of summer and some fine settled weather allowed the divers to work unhindered on the wreck, but not until the first weeks of July could lifting operations commence. Careful plans had been made including the use of models, to decide the disposition of the lifting craft, and a programme worked out by Admiral-Superintendent the Honourable A. Foley who had three staff captains and over 400 men on the site.

They began pinning down the lifting vessels at three o'clock on Tuesday morning, July 2nd. There were four lifting vessels employed, the *Wave* and *Swan*, both gunboats, and two larger ships HMS *Pearl*, a corvette and *HMS Rinaldo*, a sloop. Water ballast was let into these ships to sink them about three feet below their normal waterline. Low tide was at 5.45 am when all steel wire hawsers and chain cables attached to the wreck were hove taut. At 6.30 am the task of pumping out the four lifting craft was started by tugs moored alongside, with the addition of two Merryweather steam fire pumps on the *Pearl* and *Rinaldo*.

When the pumping had started the wind was moderate northeasterly and the sea calm, but after two hours the wind had shifted to east north east and a nasty ground swell set in. By eight o'clock conditions had worsened and the after lifting chain of the *Swan* snapped, making it necessary to slip the others to prevent the gun boat overturning. The sea became so choppy that at 8.45 am it was necessary to ease the hawsers, and shortly afterward all hawsers and chains were slipped and the whole salvage fleet returned to harbour. While slipping moorings the *Swan* was damaged in a collision with one of the tugs and a seaman injured.

It was not until Monday, July 15th that the four vessels and their attendant tugs returned to the wreck and re-positioned to begin again the long hard task of picking up the lifting wires and securing them to the four ships. This time wire hawsers were used in every position; chains were not to be trusted. Again the lifting craft were flooded and the wires tightened as the tide fell and at six am pumping started.

Meanwhile *HMS Thunderer*, an iron clad turret ship of 9,190 tons, arrived from Portland to tow the *Eurydice* into shallow water when lifted. The sterns of *Wave* and *Swan* faced each other across the wreck and *Pearl* and *Rinaldo* lay alongside. An interesting technical detail was the use of a rubberised fabric bag inflated with compressed air giving a lift of 50 tons. It was called a Popov bag, after its inventor, a Russian admiral. Initial investigations by the divers had shown that the sunken hull was embedded in the seabed by about ten feet, so repeated lifts would be needed on successive tides to successfully float it.

At one o'clock the next morning the second stage began and ballast water was again let into the waiting lifting craft. It had to be a carefully controlled procedure, no less than 900 tons of water being pumped into *HMS Pearl* alone. This flooded her hold to a depth of ten feet and sank her by five feet six inches. *HMS Rinaldo* sank five feet with 600 tons of water aboard. The two smaller vessels were each ballasted with 190 tons.

All this was accomplished with less than an hour to spare before dead low water at six o'clock. As soon as the tide turned the steam fire engine pumps on *Pearl* and *Rinaldo* were set to work, shortly followed by the pumps on the tugs moored alongside each vessel. *Wave* and *Swan* were pumped out by a single tug. Meanwhile the Popov air bag was receiving compressed air but its contribution to the total lift is impossible to estimate. With a tide rise of ten feet and about five feet from the four lifting ships it was hoped that eight or nine days would see the *Eurydice* in shallow water to allow the removal of bodies while preparations for the tow into Portsmouth Harbour were carried out.

By eight o'clock the green seaweed on the masts could be seen just below the surface and by nine o'clock all the water ballast had been pumped from the four salvage ships. Everything had gone splendidly and *HMS Thunderer* was at hand to take up her towing task. Then suddenly, chaos replaced order. Two wire hawsers had been made ready on the *Thunderer* when the strongly running tide swept her foul of some moorings and she lost all the towing gear overboard. This caused some delay while a boat's crew swept the sea bed with grapples to find the tows. Although they recovered one a diver had to be sent down for the other, but meanwhile it was decided to dispense with the second wire and substitute a heavy rope in its place, but as *HMS Thunderer* steamed to take up her position the temporary capstan fell overboard taking the entire rope cable with it. According to one report *Thunderer* now became useless for all practical purposes that day.

She seems to have been an accident prone ship. A year earlier she was visited by Queen Victoria, accompanied as usual by the faithful

The paddle tug *Grinder* in attendance as the *Eurydice* is re-floated (Gordon Phillips) and **below**
After raising her from the sea bed preparations are made to float her, upright (Carisbrooke Castle Museum)

John Brown. After the visit the Queen wrote in her journal: 'When we went on board the *Thunderer*, on August the 12th, at Osborne, Brown had fallen through an open place inside the turret, and got a severe hurt on the shin'.

Meanwhile experiments were going on to check the buoyancy of the *Eurydice*. The hawsers from the lifting ships were drawn up taut but the wreck seemed immovable. Then suddenly the load on the lifting capstans slackened and the masts of the sunken ship were seen to move. A great cheer arose from the watching seamen. Divers were sent down and reported that the sunken ship had been shifted out of her hole and moved by the tide almost a hundred feet, so that she was now resting on a firm bottom. For the remainder of that week the pattern of flooding down, pumping out and towing was repeated day after day, working at all hours as the tides demanded.

By Monday of the following week *HMS Eurydice* was in shallow water off Redcliff in Sandown Bay where the depth of water at high tide was only twenty-five feet. As the tide fell on Monday afternoon more and more of the ship was exposed until the whole of the upper deck was uncovered. Satisfaction at raising the ship must have been subdued by the unpleasant consequences. The smell arising from the dead lying between decks, combined with a variety of other deposits, was extremely offensive and many of the wreck party succumbed. While a strong team began clearing the upper deck of the debris that littered it, volunteers entered the tween deck and coffined fifteen dead who were found there. In this task the sailors were joined by a couple of civilian undertakers who gave advice and a helping hand where necessary. The grim task was not helped by the crowds of ghoulish spectators who flocked out in a host of pleasure craft. Screens were erected in the hope of denying the spectators a glimpse of the coffins as they were loaded on waiting tenders.

Before further salvage efforts could be made the open ports had to be closed. Because it was not then possible to get onto the gundeck the ports had to be blocked from outside the ship. Large square covers, made of elm and covered with felt, heavily daubed with tallow, were fitted over the ports and secured with strongbacks. As that work proceeded, the entries through the upper deck were also battened down in a similar fashion.

On Thursday, August 1st a seaman's body was washed ashore at Whitecliff. His clothing identified him as W. Shuker and his grave

111

and memorial are in Christchurch graveyard at Sandown where six more of his shipmates subsequently washed ashore are also buried. Seven more who were never identified have a memorial at Hildyards cemetery between Shanklin and Lake.

Although it was necessary to keep the public at arm's length, distinguished visitors were welcomed by the Navy. On Monday August 5th the Royal Yacht *Osborne* steamed into Sandown Bay and brought up near the *Eurydice*. On board were the Prince (later King Edward VII) and Princess of Wales with their children; the Princes Albert and George (the future King George V), both in naval cadet uniform and the Princesses, Louise, Victoria and Maud. The Prince of Wales, with others of the party, crossed to the wreck in one of *Osborne's* boats and was received by the officers in charge. The Prince stayed on the wreck for some time before leaving to return in the Royal Yacht to Osborne House.

Because of the exposed position off Redcliff in which the *Eurydice* lay, plans were made to shift her around Culver Cliff into a more sheltered area. *Pearl* and *Rinaldo* were laid alongside each side of her and secured to cables passing under her hull. To prevent the two ships heeling over towards *Eurydice* under the very heavy load, *Wave* and *Swan* were made fast outside of the others as counter-balances. The rising tide lifted the *Eurydice* in the now familiar pattern and two government tugs, *Camel* and *Grinder*, took the whole assembly in tow. The little flotilla, all ships tied together, proceeded around the eastern end of the island and into St. Helens Roads where the *Eurydice* was grounded once more. While beached off St. Helens another fifteen bodies were removed, including that of the man in the cells. The total dead recovered up to that point was 121, far fewer than expected. The number of men washed out to sea by the strong tides being greater than was first supposed.

The Prince of Wales made another visit on August 24th, this time bringing the King of Denmark (his father-in-law) and his two cadet sons in *HMS Thunderer*. Admiral Fanshawe's steam pinnace from Portsmouth transferred the royal party to *Eurydice*. A brief visit was paid below and the salvage operations were explained. The visitors then returned to *HMS Thunderer* and headed for Cowes.

On Sunday, September 1st *HMS Eurydice* was at last towed into Portsmouth Harbour; around her bow a large black mourning drape. The ill-fated vessel was laid alongside the hulk *Laurel* in Porchester

HMS Eurydice beached off Redcliff, Sandown Bay, after she had been raised in 1878 (Carisbrooke Castle Museum)

Creek and because of the attentions of the general public the Royal Marines had to mount a day and night guard.

With the ship now upright, floating and in harbour it was possible to examine her more fully. Damage was much greater than had been anticipated. The centre of the upper deck was completely missing and every other deck littered and almost choked with debris of every description. The starboard side of the lower deck had been lifted several feet as a result of the rough seas slamming the sunken ship on the bottom. Right aft on the lower deck was situated the bread room from which an intolerable stench emanated from decomposed bread, biscuit and other provisions. It was easier to get volunteers to remove the remains of the dead rather than to enter the breadroom. Men would be ill for days if their duties took them into the area. The hold was at first impossible to enter as it was half full of water and blocked with everything movable within the vicinity of the entry ways. While making room for pump suction pipes to go down into the hold the divers found a small body jammed in the wreckage. It was the bread-room boy.

As soon as the wreck was cleared dockyard workers descended on her and in a few weeks she was completely dismantled; nothing remained. *HMS Eurydice* the ship was gone forever. Only memories and questions remained. The questions were never answered. It is doubtful if they were ever adequately asked.

The only official inquiry into the loss of one of Her Majesty's ships with three hundred young trainees was the naval court martial. According to the custom of the Royal Navy the senior survivors of a shipwreck, no matter what their position, are court martialled. It is not always the best procedure for investigating a matter of public concern.

So on Tuesday, August 27th the court martial convened on board *HMS Duke of Wellington* at Portsmouth with Admiral Fanshawe, C in C, presiding. The unfortunate Able Seaman Benjamin Cuddiford and Ordinary Seaman Sidney Fletcher were formally charged with the loss of their ship. To obviate the necessity for them to appear they had already made sworn statements at the Admiralty and these were read to the Court. Oral evidence was given by observers who had seen *HMS Eurydice* passing Ventnor, and several witnesses were examined about the snowstorm, but the court elucidated little that had not been heard at the inquest, although the proceedings lasted until Monday,

114

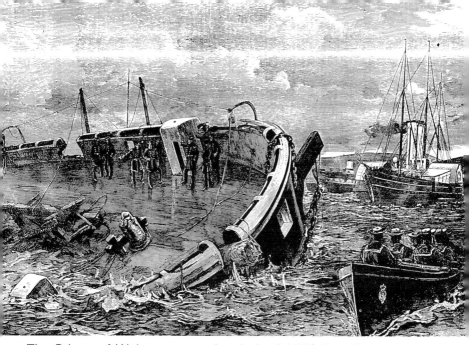

The Prince of Wales surveys the deck of *HMS Eurydice*, as depicted in the Illustrated London News on August 17th 1878.

September 2nd. The findings were: 'that Her Majesty's Ship, *Eurydice*, foundered on the afternoon of the 24th of March, 1878, by pressure of wind upon her sails during a sudden and exceptionally dense snow storm which overtook her when the approach was partially hidden by the proximity of the ship to high land'.

Although the summing up dealt in turn with other factors which could have contributed to the loss, including the open ports on the lower deck, the quality of seamanship displayed by Captain Marcus Hare, the ship's stability, all in their turn were dismissed from having anything to do with it. The verdict acquitting Cuddiford and Fletcher was of course as much a formality as charging them in the first place and any who might have been censured were either dead or not on trial.

Were the authorities certain, with their unbounded Victorian confidence that they had got to the root of the matter? Or was there a cover-up in which the Admiralty was looking after its own gold braided sons? Was the vital water ballast in the lower tier tanks missing? And did Hare know he had a cranky ship when he ordered more sail to be set? We shall never know. Perhaps Dean Stanley of Westminster, had the truth of it when he said in his sermon at a memorial service for the dead of the *Eurydice*: 'The calamities of this world, so it would seem, come not by accident, but by fixed laws, by a combination of causes, which on looking back seem irresistible'.

Or did Gerard Manley Hopkins, with a poet's perception come nearer the truth in the verses he was moved to write on the tragedy?

> *Too proud, too proud, what a press she bore!*
> *Royal, and all her royals wore,*
> *Sharp with her, shorten sail!*
> *Too late, lost, gone with the gale.*

But at least we are entitled to ask what lessons were learned from this disaster? None it would seem. The very next year *HMS Atalanta* (formerly the frigate *Juno* built in 1844 and converted to a training ship in 1878) sailed from Portsmouth with a crew of trainees. One of them was Philip Fisher, brother of the famous future Admiral Jacky Fisher. She disappeared without trace and with the loss of all hands.

Memorial to the crew of *HMS Eurydice* at Hildyards cemetery, Shanklin (author's collection)

Memorial to seven of the victims of the *Eurydice* tragedy in Christ Church burial ground, Sandown, where their bodies were washed ashore (author's collection)

4

Ships In Collision

Even the largest of ships seem dwarfed by the immensity of the sea that it sometimes seems strange that ships should so often get in each other's way at all. Yet despite modern aids to safety and navigation, collisions at sea still occur with some regularity and considerable expense. Quite recently in Isle of Wight waters was the unforgettable sight of the 42,000 ton tanker *Pacific Glory* burning in Sandown Bay after colliding with the *Allegro*. On a fine starry night in October 1970 those two large ships, in full view of each other and with plenty of sea room, managed to collide because at a crucial moment nobody on either ship was keeping a good look out.

And what of the *Andrea Doria* and the *Stockholm*? These two passenger liners, *Andrea Doria* on her maiden voyage, were steaming on a reciprocal course off the Massachusetts coast, each watching the other on its radar set. With half the Atlantic Ocean in which to manoeuvre they failed to avoid each other. It was this tragic accident in 1956 that spawned the scornful phrase 'radar assisted collision'.

If in these high-technology times such disasters can happen, how much more likely were they when seamen could rely only on their own eyes and ears. Collision has certainly always been one of the most common and terrifying of accidents at sea, as we can judge from some of the following incidents.

Pacific Glory on fire in Sandown Bay after colliding with *Allegro* in October 1970 (The News, Portsmouth)

Cambrian Princess and Alma 1902

The South Western Railway Company's steam packet *Alma*, finished loading thirty five passengers and the Continental mails and left Southampton for Le Havre shortly after midnight on April 1st 1902. The weather was wild with a heavy sea running and the Solent enveloped in haze and almost incessant rain. It was a slow journey down Southampton Water and out through the Eastern Solent; not until half past two did *Alma* clear the Nab Tower light and head out into the open channel.

Forward, in the eyes of the ship, the foul-weather lookout, wrapped in his bulky oilskins, peered into the darkness around him. He was startled to suddenly see a large sailing ship ahead, moving across the track of the steamer. The vessel was a barque, the *Cambrian Princess*, laden with guano and inward bound to Antwerp from Peru. With her crew of twenty two she had been 124 days at sea.

The watching seaman gave a warning shout but was unheard on that stormy night. With a terrific crash the *Alma* tore into the starboard quarter of the sailing ship, almost lifting her out of the water. For some minutes the two vessels were locked together, and then with a thunderous rending of timber and iron plating the barque broke away, and heeling over to port disappeared beneath the surface of the raging sea.

Although the interval between the collision and the sinking of the *Cambrian Princess* was brief there was time for the crew of the *Alma* to throw lifelines and eight men were rescued including the master, Captain Roberts. Three others were about to clamber aboard the *Alma* but the mainmast of the sailing ship came down and swept them away into the sea as they were almost within grasp of the hands waiting to save them. The *Alma*'s boat was launched and searched the area for over an hour, finding three more men who were dragged half drowned from the water. Eleven men were thus saved in total.

On the *Alma*, passengers rudely awakened by the shock of the collision rushed onto the upper deck in great alarm. But although the *Alma*'s bows were badly damaged and water was entering into the forepeak, all the watertight doors had been promptly closed and she was in no immediate danger of sinking. After standing by until all hope was past of finding more of the missing men, she steamed slowly back to Southampton, arriving about seven o'clock in the morning.

A survivor from the barque said that as soon as the haze had thickened Captain Roberts had ordered sail to be shortened and the navigation lamps to be lit. Nobody had seen the *Alma* approaching. 'Our vessel shook from stem to stern and the oncoming steamer seemed to have bitten right into us; very much as a bulldog would hold a victim with his jaws. This gave some of us time to scramble over the side of the steamer' said the survivor.

Was it then just bad luck that caused two ships' paths to cross like that on a night of poor visibility? Ill fate will be seen as not the only cause if we ask ourselves two questions. Firstly, why was the *Cambrian Princess* in that particular position, and secondly, how was it she was struck on the starboard quarter?

A half dozen miles off the Isle of Wight was no place for a sailing ship heading for Antwerp from South America. The *Cambrian Princess* should have been well out, almost in mid channel, setting a course to take her safely through the Dover Straits. On a night of such poor visibility the farther out from land she was the better. The other question, that of why the *Cambrian Princess* was rammed on her starboard side, also raises doubts about the track she was on. For it to be possible that she could be struck on that side, by a ship which had just cleared the Nab en route to Le Havre, the *Cambrian Princess* had to be sailing the wrong way and heading straight for the Isle of Wight. After 124 days at sea and a successful entry into the English Channel, there can be no doubt that, for some unknown reason, Captain Roberts was lost, not only too close to land but heading in the wrong direction. Unable to see any further than the bows of his ship, it is likely that if the *Alma* had not hit him the ever-waiting ship-hungry shores of the Wight would have claimed him anyway.

The *Cambrian Princess* was owned by W. Thomas and Company of Liverpool. She was 1,275 tons, built in 1877 in Southampton. Her last voyage had been Captain Roberts' first as her master. One hopes that his career from that ill beginning was a little more successful.

Costa Rica 1871

Most accounts of maritime disasters reveal the heroism of rescuers and it is rare indeed to come across heartless disregard for the plight of disaster victims such as happened in the rather strange story of the ramming and sinking of the French barque *Costa Rica* on December 14th 1871.

The *Costa Rica* had sailed from Le Havre, bound for Buenos Aires, under the command of Captain Olivry and carrying a few French and Italian passengers in addition to her general cargo. About midnight on a dark and windy night, an unknown, large, fully rigged sailing ship, carrying no lights, ran head-on to the *Costa Rica's* bow. The French barque's bowsprit was completely ripped away, so badly damaging her bows that water poured in.

Captain Olivry, and other men who could speak English, repeatedly hailed the stranger, appealing to those on board her not to leave them. Such entreaties either were not heard or else ignored and the mystery ship, seemingly little damaged by the collision, hauled away and made off into the darkness, leaving the sinking barque and its people to their fate.

In the little time remaining everything that was loose and would float was thrown overboard to provide something to cling to if they had to jump overboard. However help was at hand in the shape of a scruffy little collier brig from Sunderland. Her name was *Eclipse* and she was commanded by a man with a fine sturdy name, Captain Rock.

Captain Rock was on deck and taking a last look around before going below, when he heard to windward the crash of a collision. Until that moment he was unaware of any other ships in the vicinity. Captain Rock instantly ordered the helm to be put down and he beat his ship to windward in a series of short tacks, all hands peering into the darkness. *Eclipse* arrived at the scene just in time to see the unknown ship, also with her bowsprit carried away, bearing away to the south east, the blackness of the night effectively shielding her identity. The *Costa Rica* was rapidly sinking by the bows and *Eclipse* at once lowered her boats, which had been swung out ready for use.

Before the boats could reach the sinking ship she went down and the rescuers were left searching amongst the floating spars, hen coops and other flotsam for survivors. They remained on the spot for two and a half hours, and left only after everything floating had been examined. Although seventeen persons were missing, eighteen had been rescued and they were taken to Portsmouth. Indignation was aroused when news of the collision and the conduct of the mystery ship became public. One report supposed her to have been 'an English ship of large tonnage, homeward bound'. If that much was true, and we do not know that it was, then the offending ship, damaged as described by Captain Rock, must surely have been easily traceable. Who could have a vested interest in not putting a name to her?

There are other puzzling aspects to this affair. One concerns the boats of the *Costa Rica* which nowhere are mentioned. The French barque must have carried some, possibly four, and the usual positions were two amidships, inboard on the gratings, and two aft, one on each quarter. This would be well away from the collision damage, so why didn't the crew lower away a couple of boats as they had time to do? From the late 1790's it was usual to lodge the quarter boats on chocks between davits with the falls already made on so it was a simple and speedy operation. And why was time wasted by shouting, especially in English when they were French? Did the captain of *Costa Rica* know the strange ship to be English? And if he knew that much did he also know her name, but have a reason for silence?

H.M.S. "GLADIA
Rammed by S.S."S* PA
during a Snow
and became a total
off Yarmouth
25 April

HMS Gladiator, ironclad cruiser built in 1896, as she looked when she set off on her final fatal voyage in 1906 (Carisbrooke Castle Museum)

HMS Gladiator shortly after the collision with the *SS St Paul* in a snowstorm in the Solent. An unlaunched lifeboat is jammed in the davits (Carisbrooke Castle Museum)

St Paul and HMS *Gladiator* 1908

Spring was slow in coming to the South of England and the Isle of Wight in 1908. The cold winter weather had continued and deep snow still covered much of the Island. On April 25th *HMS Gladiator*, 5750 tons displacement, a second class fleet cruiser, under the command of Captain Walter Lumsden, steamed slowly through the Needles Channel on her way to Portsmouth. At the same time, outward bound from Southampton, the 11,629 ton liner *St Paul*, owned by the International Mercantile Marine Company, with Captain Frederick Maclean Passon and Trinity House pilot George Bower on the bridge, steamed at ten knots towards the narrow Hurst Channel. She was keeping carefully to the deep water channel as on either side the water shoals rapidly and her size, 554 ft long and 63 ft beam, left the liner little room for manoeuvre.

The weather, which until then had been dull and misty with recurrent snow flurries, took a decided turn for the worse. Heavy snow began to obscure the bridge and wheelhouse windows of both ships and the wind became anything but the light to moderate southwesterly breeze of that day's Met. Office forecast. As the two ships neared each other the wind was up to gale force from the north-west, driving the snow before it in a blizzard in which visibility was almost zero.

On the bridge of the *St Paul* with Captain Passon and the pilot were the chief officer and the third and fourth officers. A quartermaster was at the wheel and another, as a special look-out, was up in the crow's nest. The first officer and an able seaman were on the bows, in the 'eyes' of the ship as foul-weather lookouts. It is quite clear that the potentially hazardous situation was fully recognised and an extra good lookout was being kept. The presence of a warship in the channel ahead was at this time unknown.

On *HMS Gladiator* Captain Lumsden had not left the bridge since sailing from Portland at 10.30 am. As the ironclad passed through the Hurst Channel about 2.30 pm there were with him on the bridge, Lieutenant Mainguy, Quartermaster Lowman was at the wheel assisted by A B Watson, A B Pearson and Paskins were starboard and port lookouts. A B Spencer was messenger and A B Johnson was at the engine room telegraphs. Up on the chart house roof were a Yeoman of

125

Signals with an assistant. In the starboard chains a petty officer and a seaman were standing by with a sounding lead and another look-out was stationed forward.

Both ships it would seem were well prepared for an emergency, so why did the SS *St Paul* smash into *HMS Gladiator*, sinking her with the loss of twenty-seven naval personnel? It looks as if the cause can be summed up in just one word: confusion, but no-one was ever blamed.

Since the middle of the 19th century the conduct of ships meeting each other has been governed by The International Regulations for Preventing Collisions at Sea. They have altered since in detail only to meet 20th century conditions, but the basic rules for ships approaching each other remain as they were then. They include the signals ships must make to each other to indicate their intentions. According to Rule 28, (in the modern version it is Rule 34), one short blast of the syren is to mean 'I am altering my course to starboard', two short blasts is to mean 'I am altering my course to port' and three short blasts is to mean 'my engines are going astern'.

When Passon first saw *HMS Gladiator* through the snow she was less than half a mile away, hardly five of his own ship's lengths. The warship was very fine, about five degrees, off his bow to port. The two ships at that moment were port to port, but because of poor visibility Captain Passon could not determine the cruiser's heading. His reaction was swift, he immediately stopped his engines. But of course a ship of that size would carry her way for a very considerable distance.

Then, as Captain Passon testified at the inquest: 'I saw a puff of steam and heard one blast. We put the rudder to starboard and went full speed astern with the starboard engine. We answered with one blast which meant we were going to starboard'. He had made the right move and the right signal and would expect the other ship now to be turning to starboard, so they would be going away from each other. But even as the SS *St Paul* started her turn to starboard *HMS Gladiator* turned to port into the liner's path. Passon instantly ordered the port engine full astern power in an attempt to stop his ship, but there was too little room and too little time.

On the *Gladiator*'s bridge Captain Lumsden also first saw the *St Paul* looming out of the driving snow when she was about half a mile away. But from that moment onwards almost everything he observed differs from or contradicts Passon's account, as the transcript of his evidence at the inquest shows.

126

Administrative County of the Isle of Wight.

SUMMONS FOR Juryman ON CORONER'S INQUISITION.

By virtue of a Warrant under the hand and seal of Francis

A. Joyce Esquire, the Deputy Coroner for this County, you are hereby summoned personally to appear before him as a Juryman, on the 28th day of April, 190 6, at Two of the clock in the Afternoon precisely, at the house of Mr. Arthur Rann known by the sign of the Golden Hill in the Parish of Water in the said County, then and there to enquire on His Majesty's behalf touching the death of Reverand & others of fail not at your peril.

Dated the 27th day of April 1905

Jas Merwett Bough J. Water

of the Parish of

To Mr. Capt. Alexander

(Name and Rank of
Officer, I.W.C.)

Lumsden Almost immediately she sounded two blasts which indicated she had on port rudder.

Question Is that correct?

Lumsden That is what I wrote down. I have various evidence as to that. There is a lot of other evidence which says there was only one blast.

Question If there was a single blast what would be the object?

Lumsden A single long blast means a steamer in thick weather. It does not give any indication of whether she is going to port or otherwise. If she sounds two blasts that means she is altering her course to port. [Why did Lumsden assume he was being asked about a long single blast when short blasts were under discussion?]

Question You are not sure whether she gave one blast or otherwise?

Lumsden No, as far as I myself am concerned I did not hear any blast at all, but I observed her slowing to port.

Question If she had given two blasts instead of one her turn to port would have been in obedience to that?

Lumsden Yes, Ordinary signalman Davis reported it.

Question What did you do when you saw her turn to port?

Lumsden The order was given to put on 30 degrees of port rudder.

Question The effect of it would be that you would go to port?

Lumsden Yes.

Question On which side did you mean to pass the *St Paul*?

Lumsden I intended to pass her on her starboard side.

Here Captain Lumsden could very well have looked in serious trouble. Rule 18 of the International Regulations says: 'When two steam vessels are meeting end on, or nearly end on, so as to involve risk of collision, each shall alter her course to starboard, so that each may pass on the port side of the other'. The same obligation is embodied in Rule 14 of the modern version. This was an inquest and no-one was on trial but any evidence coming to light might obviously be seized on at any subsequent proceedings. Lumsden was saved from enmeshing himself further by a knowledgeable and sympathetic juror, a Captain H Cross, who reminded him that he had a right to refuse to give evidence which might incriminate him. Lumsden replied: 'Then I will withhold it'. So he was saved from explaining why he had given the seemingly wrong helm order, or if he had mis-heard or misunderstood the steamer's sound signals.

The *St Paul* cut deeply into *HMS Gladiator* at the forward end of the after boiler room. Lumsden at once ordered his engines full astern (another questionable order?) but the cruiser remained firmly entangled. After a minute or so, Lumsden stopped engines, hailed the bridge of the *St Paul* and called for the liner to go astern, which she did, breaking free from the *Gladiator*. Once released the cruiser was driven by the high wind and tide on to the shore at Sconce Point where she grounded. A great cheer went up from her sailors when they felt her touch, for at least the risk of her foundering in deep water was eliminated. The starboard anchor was let go to make sure she stayed put, but *Gladiator* was already heeling to starboard and many of her crew were in the water, swimming for the shore. Struggling men tried to launch the boats, but although a few were got away from the starboard side before it disappeared under water, none could be freed from the port side.

After a lapse of around fifteen minutes, boats from the *St Paul* arrived and began lifting men from the water and off the capsized hull. Captain Lumsden himself was ultimately rescued by one of *St Paul*'s lifeboats, leaving his ship only when satisfied no-one else remained.

On the cliffs of Sconce Point is Fort Victoria and stationed there in 1908 were the Royal Engineers who mounted a rescue operation. Many of the soldiers earned commendation for dashing into the pounding surf and dragging to safety many of the *Gladiator*'s crew who were trying to swim ashore. Others rowed out to the cruiser in the Engineers' dinghies and racing gig, while the rest of them cared for survivors brought to the small pier by the rescue boats.

Altogether twenty seven naval ratings were drowned, trapped below as she overturned. There were no injuries on the steamer but damage to her bows was severe. A huge gash some four or five feet deep was slashed from the stem bar to a distance of about 20 ft aft. The starboard bow plating below the gash down to the ship's fore-foot was very badly buckled. On the port side of the bow a ragged, more or less round hole, had been punched through the steel plating, probably by a gun barrel. She returned slowly to Southampton for repairs.

The *St Paul* seems to have had more than its fair share of troubles. She was built by the Cramp Yard in Philadelphia and entered service on the North Atlantic in 1895, a year before the *Gladiator* was launched. A well appointed and popular ship she could carry 1,370 passengers and 400 crew. Twin screws powered by quadruple expansion steam engines with a total of 20,000 horse power gave her a comfortable service speed of nineteen knots. In November 1900 she was involved in a collision with what was believed at the time to be a submerged wreck. The tail shaft fractured and the starboard propeller disappeared into the deep. The starboard engine was so badly damaged it had to be completely rebuilt. In 1918, ten years after the tragic collision with *HMS Gladiator*, the *St Paul* capsized in Manhattan Docks, New York. She had been re-named *Knoxville* and was undergoing conversion to a troop transport for the United States Navy. Although refloated and subsequently returned to the Atlantic passenger service with her previous owners and once again as *St Paul* she was scrapped at Wilhelmshaven in 1923.

HMS Gladiator was one of four ships of the *Arrogant* class, quite a small ship of 5,750 tons displacement, launched in 1896. With a top speed of only nineteen knots she was rated as a second class fleet cruiser and led an unremarkable career until thrust briefly into the headlines in 1908. A sister ship, *HMS Vindictive*, became famous when she was used as the blockship in the famous Zeebrugge raid of May 10th 1918.

Six months after the collision, following a difficult salvage operation, *Gladiator* arrived back in Portsmouth. When built in 1896 she had cost £287,000. It was estimated that the cost of repairs would be at least £100,000, but the Admiralty had already spent about £30,000 on the salvage and the ship was already obsolete, so in the end she was scrapped.

Her tragic sinking inspired T E Mussell, a local poet who can best be described as the Isle of Wight's answer to William McGonagall (whom Punch called 'the greatest bad verse writer of his age) to pen 88 lines of indifferent rhyme. He sent a copy to King Edward VII who 'accepted it with pleasure', although it is difficult to see how the King could find pleasure in being reminded about the loss of one of his ships in circumstances which might have been avoidable.

In June 1908 Captain Lumsden faced a court martial on a charge of hazarding his ship. Like the *Eurydice* court martial it seems to have been none too searching and though he was found guilty he suffered nothing worse than a severe reprimand. For him it was stated that the *SS St. Paul* was going too fast in the snow, but it is significant that the High Court threw out an Admiralty claim against International Mercantile Marine for damages.

Salvage operations on *HMS Gladiator* in progress. Straining wires lead back to the shore to pull her upright as compressed air 'camels' provide lift from the seaward side and **below** the damage to her starboard side seen after she had been dry docked (Carisbrooke Castle Museum)

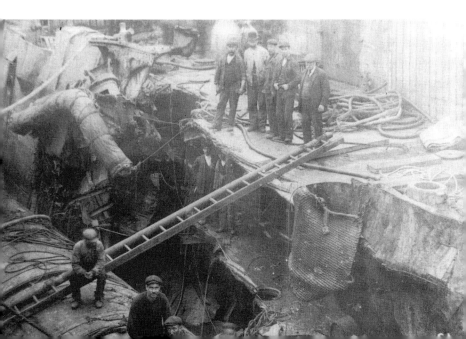

The *Empress Queen* wrecked on Bembridge Ledge, 1916
(Gordon Phillips)

5

Island Waters In
Two World Wars

The two world wars of this century added greatly to the toll of ship losses round Isle of Wight shores. In the combined total of ten years at least eighty-four ships, of all types, were sunk within the waters of the Wight. These are all identified, but there could well be many more yet to be discovered, due to the censorship regulations in force at the time.

To relate all these losses in detail would be tedious, but enough will be examined to paint a fair picture of the wartime dangers of the Island shipping lanes, which led to the sinking of fifty one ships in the First World War and thirty-three in the 1939–45 conflict.

Not all wartime mishaps were due to enemy action. The normal everyday hazards that attend sea-going were still present and took their toll. In 1914–18 four ships ran aground, and probably would have done so, war or no war. Three of them were eventually refloated but the fourth, the paddle steamer *Empress Queen* impaled herself on Bembridge Ledge on Febuary 1st 1916 and what remains of her is still there. Only one ship came ashore in the Second World War. In November 1939 a Royal Navy vessel, the *Britisher*, ran on to the Ship Ledge but fortunately suffered little damage and was soon refloated.

The torpedo gunboat *HMS Hazard* sunk after a collision with the *SS Western Australia* in January 1918 (Gordon Phillips)

HMS Boxer sunk after collision with *SS Patrick*

Much more costly in terms of ships and men were collisions. In the First World War seven ships were lost off the Island by that cause, but in the six years of the Second World War only two ships were sunk as a result of such accidents.

The first and most disastrous collision with regard to loss of life was the sinking of the troopship *Mendi* on January 21st 1917, drowning over 600 men of the South African Native Labour Corps. She was in collision with the 11,000 ton *Darro* and sank in twenty minutes. The *Camswan* went down on October 19th the same year after colliding with *SS Polbrae*. *Myrtlegrove* was another collision victim the next month.

January 28th the next year saw the loss of the 1,070 ton destroyer *HMS Hazard* which sank as a result of a collision with the *SS Western Australia*. Only eleven days later the Royal Navy lost another destroyer of the same 1894 vintage, *HMS Boxer* which came off worst when in collision with *SS St Patrick*.

The collision between the *War Knight* and the *O B Jennings* on March 24th 1918 must have been a spectacular affair as the *O B Jennings* was carrying naphtha which ignited and eventually exploded, setting fire to the *War Knight* and killing thirty two of that unfortunate ship's crew. Out of control and burning fiercely *War Knight* was sunk just off Freshwater Bay by a torpedo fired from a Royal Navy destroyer. The *O B Jennings* meanwhile, also on fire, was towed into Sandown Bay to allow her cargo to burn itself out. There, like a candle flame attracting moths, she attracted the enemy and while still on fire but afloat she was torpedoed some days later by a German U-Boat. She was refloated and repaired and eventually sailed in convoy to America, but a hundred miles out from New York she was again torpedoed and this time sank for ever.

The last collision of the war to be noted was on April 3rd, 1918, when the 600 ton *France Amiee* had the misfortune to be hit by *HMS P35*, a P class patrol boat. The 'P' class boats were of 613 tons and had ram bows of hardened steel and not surprisingly the *France Amiee* and her cargo of coal quickly sank.

The two ships lost by collision in the Second World War were the *Edenwood*, rammed by the *Derbyshire* on Christmas Day 1939 and the drifter *Charde* which had been taken into naval service.

When we turn to enemy action the most effective weapon on both sides contributing to ship losses was undoubtedly the mine. In

135

European waters during the Second World War the German forces laid 226,000 mines, while Great Britain exceeded that number with 262,000 mines laid.

During the First World War eleven ships were lost to mines within our area. This number includes an 'own goal', the German submarine *UB-81* on December 1st 1917. The first British vessel mined was the destroyer *HMS Velox* on October 25th 1915. She was built in 1902 by Hawthorn Leslie and belonged to the 'C' class – despite her name. A small ship, *HMS Velox* was only 420 tons although capable of 30 knots.

The only loss by a mine in 1916 was the *SS Algerian* 3,837 tons but the next year was a bad one. The *Lowmount* with a cargo of iron ore went down on May 7th 1917 and three more ships, the *Camberwell*, *Lucknow* and the *Elford* were all sunk in one day, May 18th. Then the *Corbett Woodall*, mined on May 30th ended a disastrous period attributed to the mine-laying submarine *UC 36*. The year ended in another spate of sinkings with the *Oriflam*, on November 25th, the *Brigitta*, 2084 tons, on December 4th and the *Apley*, a trawler in naval service on December 6th.

Losses due to mines were also very unevenly spread throughout the Second World War. The last definite mine victim was the *Sargasso*, a sailing ship of 223 tons on June 6th 1943. The first was the boom defence vessel *Cambrian* on May 30th 1940, followed a few days later by the motor vessel *Capable*, 216 tons, on June 5th and *Campeadore* on June 22nd.

One sinking came to light only recently as this book was in preparation, some 43 years after the event. Isle of Wight diver Mr Martin Woodward, director of the Bembridge Maritime Museum, found the wreckage of the submarine *HMS Swordfish* off St. Catherine's Point in 150 feet of water. The *Swordfish* left Gosport on November 7th 1940 and disappeared without trace. There is no doubt she struck a mine and sank with all of her crew of 40 officers and ratings. This disaster was quickly followed by the loss of another warship and strangely her resting place has also been discovered by Martin Woodward. *HMS Acheron*, on trials after a refit, was steaming off the Wight when she too struck a mine. The 1,350 ton destroyer, her bows blown off sank like a stone, taking 151 members of her crew with her. Only 15 men survived that day, December 17th 1940. Both wreck sites are now designated war graves and should be free from disturbance.

Corbet Woodall sunk by a mine in 1917 while carrying coal
from Tyneside to Poole (Gordon Phillips)

The Island ferry *P. S. Portsdown* lost on September 20th 1941 after striking a mine between Portsmouth and Ryde (E. D. Payne)

Unfortunate consequences attended the sinking of the vintage paddle tug *Irishman* on May 8th 1941 as she took with her a small grab dredger, the *Percy* and a lighter which were alongside. The following month saw the sinking of the Norwegian ship *Ala* June 13th 1941.

A particular blow to Isle of Wight inhabitants was sinking of the paddle steamer *Portsdown*, the Southern Railway ferry which hit a mine on September 20th 1941 as she ran the four am trip from Portsmouth to Ryde. This early morning sailing was known as 'the mail boat' and was much used by servicemen on leave. About ten minutes after leaving Portsmouth Harbour *Portsdown* struck a mine, blowing off her bow section which rolled over and sank. The other and larger part of the ship remained afloat in fairly shallow water. Luckily there were only about forty people on board of whom, perhaps, some thirty were servicemen. Rescue services from Portsmouth found twenty-four survivors. This means that at least nineteen people died, although only three bodies were later recovered.

Then for a whole year the waters of the Wight, it seems, were free of ship losses. None can be found for 1942 from any war activity whatever. it was not until January 12th 1943 that the *Kingston Jacinth* hit a mine and sank. Apart from the *Sargasso* she was the last mine victim around the Wight.

When we come to examine sinkings by submarine launched torpedoes a considerable difference between the two wars becomes apparent. In the First World War twenty three ships were torpedoed within the area, but only five were lost to this weapon in the Second World War, despite it being a longer conflict. This great disparity can be attributed to a number of reasons, one of which was the early and effective mining of the Dover Straits in the Second World War, forcing the U-Boats to take the northern route around Scotland into the Atlantic until the occupied French Channel ports could be adapted for use by German submarines. Another was of course the increased use of aircraft for maritime patrol and the immediate institution of coastal convoys.

The first sinking off the Isle of Wight in World War One credited to a German submarine did not come until very late in the war when the unlucky victim was the fleet oiler *Wapello*, torpedoed on June 15th 1917. Next ship torpedoed was the *Redesmere*, 2,133 tons whose nineteen crewmen were lost. There then followed a bad spell. *Luciston*

S.S. Cuba, an 11,000 ton French liner taken into the British war service, which was sunk by a torpedo from *U1195* on April 6th 1945 (Tom Rayner)

Highland Brigade torpedoed by a U-Boat in April 1918 (Tom Rayner)

2,877 tons, sunk on December 24th; *Espagne* on December 25th, *Fallodon* 3,011 tons, on December 28th, *Westville* on December 31st 1917, the Norwegian *Asborg* on January 3rd 1918, the French ship *Leon* on January 7th.

The *Mechanician*, 9,044 tons was lost with thirteen of her crew; torpedoed by the *UB35* on January 20th 1918. Two ships went down two days later, the Norwegian *Molina* and the 3,677 ton *Serrana*. Probably the same U-Boat sank both. Again in February two ships were torpedoed on the same day February 12th. They were the *Eleanor*, 1,980 tons; and the *Polo*, 2915 tons, both armed merchant vessels. A third vessel, the *Borgny*, a Norwegian, was sunk on February 26th.

Five ships were torpedoed in March; the Norwegian *Braat II* on the 7th, *Londonier* and *Tweed* both on the 13th; the armed merchant vessel *South Western*, 674 tons, on the 16th and the *Azemmor*, a French ship on the 20th. Before the end of hostilities in November four more ships fell victims to U-Boats. They were the *Highland Brigade*, an armed merchant vessel of 3669 tons April 7th, the *Lois* on April 12th, the armed merchant vessel *Isleworth*, 2871 tons sunk off Ventnor with the loss of twenty nine of her crew April 30th and finally the 5,815 ton *Clan Macvey* August 8th 1918.

As in the First World War, U-Boat activities did not affect the Wight until quite late in the Second World War. The first ship torpedoed was the *Prince Leopold*, a ship requisitioned for naval service. She was sunk on July 29th 1944 followed only three days later by the *St Enogat*, 2,360 tons. The *Dumfries*, 5,149 tons, was sent to the bottom on December 23rd 1944. On February 6th 1945 the 5,222 ton *Everleigh* was torpedoed at the start of a voyage to New York.

The last victim to fall to a U-Boat was also the largest sunk in Wight waters. The liner *Cuba*, built by Swan Hunter and Wigham Richardson of Newcastle for the Compagnie Générale Transatlantique had been on a voyage from Martinique to Casablanca when she was seized by the Royal Navy following the French capitulation in 1940, and after a coat of grey paint the ship was taken into service by the Ministry of Transport. She was registered at 11,420 tons. On April 6th 1945 while in convoy, en-route to Le Havre, the *Cuba* was stalked by the German submarine *U-1195* and torpedoed. One of the escort destroyers *HMS Watchman*, a V and W class veteran of 1918 successfully located and depth charged *U-1195* which lays on the bottom close to her victim.

One cause of shipwreck in the Second World War which was an entirely new factor so far as the waters of the Isle of Wight are concerned is enemy air attack. The first to go down from air attack was the *Crestflower* on July 19th 1940, followed by the *Terlings* two days later. The Dutch vessel *Ajax* was bombed and sunk on August 8th the same year and *Empire Crusader* on the same day. After a lull of almost eight months the *Wilna* was sent to the bottom by enemy aircraft on March 24th 1941 and the *Dagmar* on June 9th.

The *Albert C Field* a Canadian ship carrying 2,500 tons of ammunition was hit and sunk by a torpedo launched from an aircraft of the Luftwaffe on June 18th 1944. The use of aerial torpedoes was rare around the Isle of Wight.

Other equally highly mobile and dangerous assailants were the German E-Boats. These diesel engined craft were usually larger than the Royal Navy motor torpedo boats and, initially, were faster and more heavily armed. It was a long time before British Light Coastal Forces gained parity and E-Boat crews gained the respect and grudging admiration of their adversaries for their daring and high degree of seamanship. The low profile and high speed of the craft made them difficult to combat, especially during night attacks.

Despite these advantages, E-Boats sank only two ships that we know of in Island waters, but their activities were concentrated on the east coast of Britain where from bases across the North Sea they took a continuous toll. The two ships that fell victim to E-Boats off the Island were *Ashanti* (a merchant ship, not the Tribal class destroyer), and the *Dungrange*, 600 tons, both sunk on the same day, June 10th 1944.

There were no E-Boats in the First World War but the Germans employed a method of destroying small shipping of which there is only one example round the Isle of Wight. On May 17th 1917, about eight miles south of the Needles, the *Florence Loesa* a sailing ship of 115 tons, was stopped and boarded by a party from a surfaced U-Boat. The crew was ordered into the ship's boat, and the Germans, not thinking the quarry big enough to justify the cost of a torpedo quickly destroyed it by explosive charges. This method of attack was often deployed by U-Boats against fishing and coastal vessels and led to the use of 'Q' or 'decoy' ships. These were usually small merchant ships, sometimes trawlers, with guns hidden behind dummy deckhouses or behind false bulwarks to give the impression that the little ship was defenceless. These were often successful in luring prowling U-Boats to the surface expecting an easy prize. Then down would go the deckhouse, up would go the White Ensign, and the guns would open fire. Such was the reception that accounted for the sinking of the *UB38* when she encountered the 'Q' ship *Glen* off the Island on May 17th 1917.

One other wartime wreck is worth a mention and that is the sinking of *HMS Bruce*, a Scott class destroyer built in 1918 by Cammell Laird. She was torpedoed off the Isle of Wight November 22nd 1939, not by the enemy but by the Royal Navy, deliberately.

Development of a new torpedo pistol (or detonator) which could be set off to trigger either magnetically or by impact, had reached the stage where full scale trials were necessary. The ageing destroyer was chosen as the guinea pig, and an eighteen inch Fleet Air Arm pattern torpedo was launched against her with the pistol set in the magnetic mode. Set to run under *HMS Bruce* without hitting her, the torpedo exploded exactly as planned. With her bottom blown in and back broken, she plunged to the seabed.

O. B. Jennings on fire in Sandown Bay after collision with *War Knight* which sank off Freshwater (A. J. Butler and R. G. McInnes)

Appendices

Key to Chart No. 1

No	Ship	Position	Date
1	Les Deux Amis	Grange Chine	1799
2	Clarendon	Blackgang Chine	1836
3	Victor Emmanuel	Chale Bay	1861
4	Ellen Horsfall	Grange Chine	1862
5	Cedarine	Brightstone Grange	1862
6	Lotus	Rocken End	1862
7	Sauve-Garde	Luccombe	1866
8	Tale-Baure	Sandown Bay	1866
9	Underley	Dunnose Point	1871
10	Hephzibah	Hanover Point	1871
11	Cassandra	Hanover Point	1871
12	Irex	Scratchells Bay	1890
13	George Henry	Shingles Bank	1894
14	Constance Ellen	Shingles Bank	1894
15	Alcester	Atherfield Ledge	1897
16	Eurydice	Off Luccombe	1878
17	Cambrian Princess	Off the Nab Light	1902
18	Costa Rica	South of the Wight	1871
19	Gladiator	Sconce Point	1908

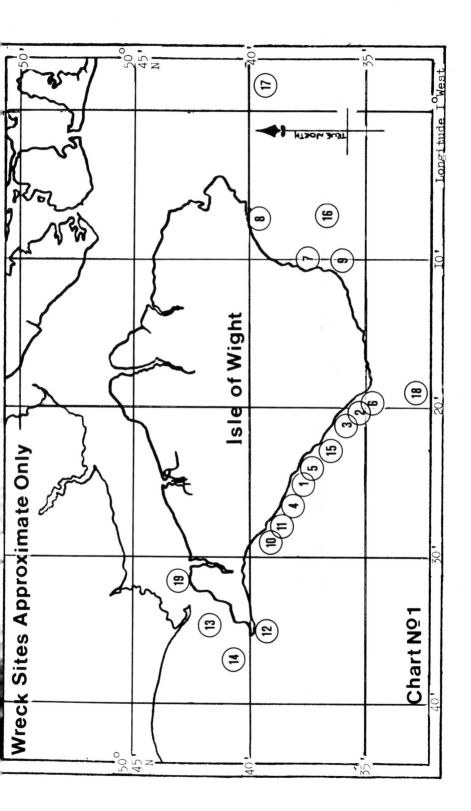

Wreck Sites Approximate Only

Isle of Wight

TRUE NORTH

Chart Nº1

Longitude 1° West

War Losses 1914–1918

Numbered in order of Incident

1. Neath
2. New Enterprise
3. Velox, HMS
4. Algerian
5. Empress Queen
6. Charlott Sophia
7. U-Boat (Unidentified)
8. Souvenier
9. Mendi
10. Low Mount
11. Florence Loesa
12. UB-39
13. Camberwell
14. Lucknow
15. Elford
16. Corbett Woodall
17. Wapello
18. Camswan
19. Redsmere
20. Snar
21. Myrtlegrove
22. Oriflamme
23. UB-81
24. Brigitta
25. Apley
26. La Peru
27. Luciston
28. Espagne
29. Fallodon
30. Westville
31. Asborg
32. Leon
33. Mechanician
34. Hazard, HMS
35. Molina
36. Serrana
37. Boxer. HMS
38. Eleanor
39. Polo
40. Borgney
41. Braat II
42. Londonier
43. Tweed
44. Southwestern
45. Azemor
46. War Knight
47. France Amiee
48. Highland Brigade
49. Luis
50. Isleworth
51. Clan Macvey

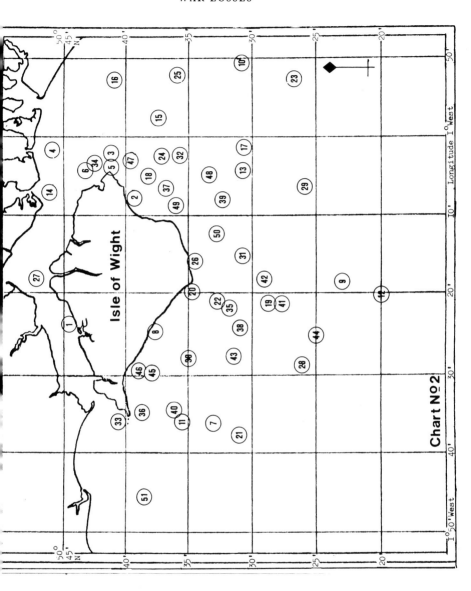

Chart No2

Isle of Wight

War Losses 1939–1945

Numbered in order of Incident

1. Britisher
2. Edenwood
3. Cambrian
4. Capable
5. Caroline Susan
6. Charde
7. Campeadore
8. Crestflower
9. Terlings
10. Ajax
11. Coquetdale
12. Empire Crusader
13. Swordfish (undisclosed position)
14. Acheron HMS
15. Stanwold
16. Wilna
17. Irishman
18. Dagmar
19. Ala
20. Portsdown
21. Kingston Jacinth
22. Sargasso
23. LCT809
24. Ashanti
25. Dungrange
26. Albert C Field
27. Prince Leopold
28. St Enogat
29. LCV P1199
30. Dumfries
31. Everleigh
32. Cuba
33. U1195

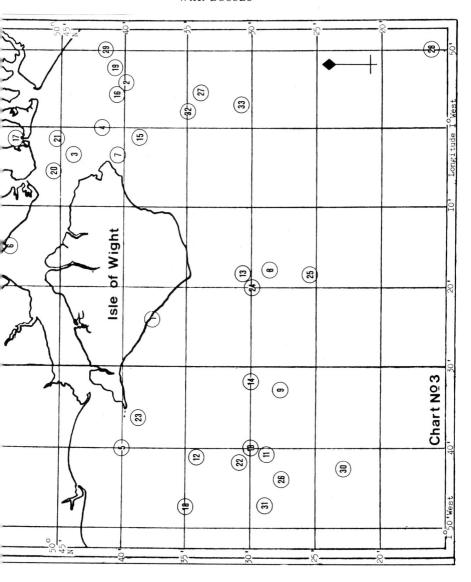

Isle of Wight

Chart NO 3

Major sources consulted for
the various ships

Les Deux Amis, ADM.1/5349/9841 1799 Isle of Wight Magazine 1799.
Clarendon, 'Wreck of the Clarendon:' (Isle of Wight C.C. Teachers Centre) Hampshire Independent 18 Oct 1836 Isle of Wight Mercury 3 Sept 1890 10 Sept 1890 'Reeds' Nautical Almanac' 1985 Directory of the Isle of Wight 1871, Navigation (Time-Life Books) 1975.
Victor Emmanuel, Hampshire Advertiser 9 Feb 1861.
Cedarine, Isle of Wight Observer 5 April 1862, Isle of Wight County Press 8 August 1931, The Times 5 April 1862
Ellen Horsfall and Lotus, Isle of Wight Observer 25 Oct 1862
Sauvé-gardé, Isle of Wight Observer 31 March 1866, 1 Sept 1866
Talé-Bauré, Isle of Wight Observer 31 March 1866, Illustrated London News 31 March 1866
Underley, The Graphic 11 Nov 1871, Isle of Wight Observer 30 Sept 1871
Hephzibah, Isle of Wight Observer 25 Nov 1871
Cassandra, Isle of Wight Observer 25 Nov 1871
Irex, Isle of Wight County Press 1 Feb 1890, Isle of Wight County Press 15 Feb 1890, Isle of Wight Observer 1 Feb 1890
George Henry and Constance Ellen, Isle of Wight County Press 17 Feb 1894, Bouquet. M. South Eastern Sail, 1840–1940 (David and Charles) 1972
Alcester, Haws A. D. Letters 2 March 1897 (Cowes Maritime Museum)
Eurydice, The Times 25 March 1878, Isle of Wight Observer Mar–Sept 1878.
Alma and Cambrian Princess, Isle of Wight Guardian 5 April 1902
Costa Rica, Isle of Wight Observer 23 Dec 1871
St. Paul and Gladiator, Isle of Wight County Press 2 May 1908, 9 May 1908, 16 May 1908, 12 Sept 1908, 10 Oct 1908

Right of Wreck A Trilogy of Greed

Hockey C. F., *Insula Vecta* (Phillmore 1982)
Prestwich M., *History Today* (Vol. 35 1985)
Hillier, George, *History and Antiquities of the Isle of Wight*. (Harison & Sons 1856)
Worsley, Richard, *History of the Isle of Wight*. (Hamilton, 1781)
Worsley Papers, Isle of Wight County Record Office *JER/WA/36/6*
Adams, Davenport, *Handbook of the Isle of Wight* (Nelson 1869)
Order of Council, 10th Charles 2nd. (*Miscellany Papers*, Carisbrooke Castle Museum)

Island Waters In Two World Wars

British Vessels lost at Sea, 1939–1945 (HMSO 1947)
Young, J., *A Dictionary of Ships of the Royal Navy of the Second World War* (Patrick Stephens 1975)
Dittmar, F. J. & Colledge, J. J., *British warships 1914–1919*. (Ian Allen 1975)
Preston, Anthony, *V and W class Destroyers 1917–1945* (Macdonald 1971)
Cooper, B., *The E-Boat Threat*. (Macdonald & Janes 1976)
Griffiths, Maurice, *The Hidden Menace*. (Conway Maritime 1981)
Le Fleming, H. M., *Warships of World War I*. (Ian Allen)
Cremer, Peter, *U 333*. (The Bodley Head 1984).

Bibliography

Country Life, *Book of Nautical Terms Under Sail*. (Hamlyn 1978)

Kemp, Peter (Ed), *Oxford Companion to Ships and the Sea*. (Oxford University Press, 1979)

Simpson, Colin, *Lusitania*. (Longman 1972)

Campbell, G. Rear Admiral, *My Mystery Ships*

Chatterton, E. K., *"Q" Ships and their story*. (1922)

Gray, Edwin, *A Damned Un-English Weapon* (Seeley, Service 1971)

du Boulay, E., *Bembridge Past and Present*. (Observer Press, Ryde I.W. 1911)

Rayner, C. T., *All my Yesterdays*. (Saunders, Shanklin I.W. 1978)

Garle, Hubert, *A Driving Tour in the Isle of Wight* (Isle of Wight County Press, 1905)

Mew, F., *Back of the Wight*. (Isle of Wight County Press, 1934)

Treanor, T. S., *The Log of a Sky Pilot*. (Religious Tract Society)

Hudson, K. & Nicholls. A., *The Book of Shipwrecks*. (MacMillan 1979)

Campbell, George F., *China Tea Clippers*. (Adlard Coles 1974)

Ayre, A. L., *Theory and Design of British Shipbuilding*. (Thomas Reed)

Lambert, Andrew, *Battleships in Transition*. (Conway Maritime Press 1984)

Hope, Ronald, *The Merchant Navy* (Stanford Maritime 1980)

Underhill, Howard, *Sailing Ship Rigs and Rigging*. (Brown Son & Ferguson Ltd. 1938)

Acknowledgements

A book of this style cannot be written without willing assistance from a great many people. I should, first of all, express my gratitude to Mr. Clifford Webster, Isle of Wight County Archivist, and Mr. Jim O'Donnell, Assistant Archivist at the Isle of Wight County Record Office, for their generously given help and guidance.

My thanks are due also to the staff of the I.W. Library Service, particularly at the Lord Louis Library, the I.W. Reference Library, Newport and the Maritime Library and Museum, Cowes. The Portsmouth City Central Library, and Liverpool City Libraries must also be included here.

Although all photographic sources are acknowledged with the illustrations, I should like to stress my gratitude to the following for their particular efforts: Roy Brinton, on behalf of the Trustees of Carisbrooke Castle Museum, Tom Rayner, Gordon Phillips, Barry Elliott, Ray Hunt, Ben Houfton and Gordon Wheeler.

My thanks also to Ron Hoverd for the chartwork, and his advice on tidal streams and coastal navigation around the Wight.

The exertions of Mrs. Maureen Turnbull and Miss Siobhan Whittington to turn my manuscript into a tidy and readable typescript must be marked by a heartfelt expression of appreciation.

Permission to photograph the name board of the *Underley* was kindly given by its owners, Mr. and Mrs. Strevens. It is a sobering thought that it is probably the only readily identifiable and indisputable relic remaining from the last hundred years of Island shipwrecks.

The painting of the ill-fated HMS *Eurydice* was executed especially for this book by my friend Robert Scott. What a splendid job he did.

I owe a deep debt of gratitude to Dr David Tomalin, the Isle of Wight County Archaeologist. It was he who first suggested to me that I should undertake the book and without his constant advice and encouragement my footsteps would have faltered long ago.

Crown copyright material in the Public Record Office, Kew, is reproduced by permission of the Controller of Her Majesty's Stationery Office.

I would like to acknowledge here also my gratitude to my wife for her forbearance during the last few years. She must be sick of the very sound of the word 'ship'.

The *New Enterprise* aground at Sandown 1914 (Gordon Phillips)

Index

Bold figures are page numbers for illustrations

158